PUTTING MARKETING IDEAS INTO ACTION

GW00630975

TO:-
FROM
GU S

DUE

13 SEP 2

2

EXTEN
DUE
RET

30 A

SUE
RE

AN

Other titles in the Successful LIS Professional series

THE SUCCESSFUL LIS PROFESSIONAL

SERIES EDITOR
Sheila Pantry

PUTTING MARKETING IDEAS INTO ACTION

Keith Hart

1999/2000
SURREY LIBRARIES

LIT   021·7

LIBRARY ASSOCIATION PUBLISHING
LONDON

© Keith Hart 1999

Published by
Library Association Publishing
7 Ridgmount Street
London WC1E 7AE

Library Association Publishing is wholly owned by The Library Association.

Except as otherwise permitted under the Copyright Designs and Patents Act 1988 this publication may only be reproduced, stored or transmitted in any form or by any means, with the prior permission of the publisher, or, in the case of reprographic reproduction, in accordance with the terms of a licence issued by The Copyright Licensing Agency. Enquiries concerning reproduction outside those terms should be sent to Library Association Publishing, 7 Ridgmount Street, London WC1E 7AE.

First published 1999

British Library Cataloguing in Publication Data
A catalogue record for this book is available from the British Library.

ISBN 1-85604-182-4

Typeset in 11/14 pt Aldine 721 by Library Association Publishing.
Printed and made in Great Britain by Bookcraft (Bath) Ltd, Midsomer Norton, Somerset.

Contents

Series Editor's preface

With rapid technological advances and new freedoms, the workplace presents a dynamic and challenging environment. It is just these advances, however, that necessitate a versatile and adaptable workforce which appreciates that lifelong full-time jobs are a thing of the past. Work is being contracted out, de-structured organizations are emerging, and different skills and approaches are required from all workers who must solve new and changing problems. These workers must become self-motivated and multi-skilled, and be constantly learning. Demonstrating the international economic importance of professional development, the European Commission has officially voiced its support for a European community committed to lifelong learning.

For the information professional, the key to success in this potentially de-stabilizing context is to develop the new skills the workplace demands. Above all, the LIS professional must actively prioritize a commitment to continuous professional development. The information industry is growing fast and the LIS profession is experiencing very rapid change. This series has been designed to help you manage change by ensuring the growth of your own portfolio of professional skills. By reading these books you will have begun the process of seeing yourself as your own best resource and accepting the rewarding challenge of staying ahead of the game.

The series is very practical, focusing on specific topics relevant to all types of library and information service. Recognizing that your time is precious, these books have been written so that they may be easily read and digested. They include instantly applicable ideas and techniques which you can put to the test in your own workplace, helping you to succeed in your job.

The authors have been selected because of their practical experience and enthusiasm for their chosen topic and we hope you will benefit from their advice and guidance. The points for reflection, checklists and summaries are designed to provide stepping stones for you to assess your understanding of the topic as you read.

In *Putting marketing ideas into action*, Keith Hart introduces LIS professionals at all levels to marketing techniques, and helps them examine where their service is now, where they would like it to be and how to start moving in the desired direction.

It will also serve as a deskbook when help is needed with specific projects, and addresses many questions such as:

➤ what is marketing?
➤ choosing and reaching your targets
➤ ways and means to get your message across
➤ evaluating your success
➤ justifying your marketing as an investment.

Keith Hart's experience as a marketing manager to a leading library supplier gives him a unique opportunity to help all LIS professionals, in whatever setting they are working.

I am sure you will benefit from reading this book and putting the ideas into action. May I wish you enjoyment and satisfaction in your endeavours to market successfully your information and library service!

Sheila Pantry

Introduction

As a professional marketeer who arrived in libraries relatively late in life, I am aware that librarians, on the whole, regard marketing with suspicion. It is a discipline belonging to another world, populated by streetwise pushers with ethics that Machiavelli would be proud of, driven only by profit and a mission to persuade you to buy things you don't need.

This situation is hardly helped by the worthy tomes on marketing that discourage active participation – perhaps they carry a 'procrastination' virus deeply embedded in the text. This is a virus that leaves your computer unaffected but ensures that everything you read about the subject is consigned to the folder in your brain labelled 'To be opened when I have the time'. Or to put it another way, when you have nothing else to do. And when was the last time that happened?

This situation is changing – libraries are becoming more proficient at identifying and satisfying the needs of their customers and, whether they like it or not, it is marketing that has helped them achieve this.

This book has been written primarily for first–time marketeers – especially for staff apprehensive about this new world and nervous about making mistakes. It aims to remove their fears and encourage them to try out marketing techniques for themselves.

Reading about marketing and not finding out how it works in your own situation is like reading a book entitled *How to swim*. It's a useful introduction, a first step pointing you in the right direction, but just because you finished the book it doesn't mean you can swim. Until you have tried it for yourself you will always be an observer.

This book aims to acclimatize you to your environment, give you some pointers and encourage you to dip your toe then the whole body into the shallow end of the pool. When you feel safe at this depth you will move into the deeper parts when you are ready.

Continuing the analogy, the exercises in the book are to be compared with the friendly swimming instructor, gently pushing you a little further into the pool until you have enough confidence to take the plunge alone.

There are many exercises and not all may be relevant to you. But think carefully before deciding to skip them. If you feel you have nothing to learn from a particular exercise then adapt it to your own situation.

Although the term 'librarian' is used throughout this book, it is meant to include everyone working in all types of library and information centre, and all organizations requiring the skills of library and information professionals. So, if you are a Library Manager, Information Centre Manager, Researcher, Information Officer, Knowledge Worker, or Cybrarian, please do not be offended. This book is for you!

Because there are many types of library, throughout the book I use four libraries as examples to illustrate different marketing situations in libraries. These are:

> ➤ a public library wanting to provide business information to small local businesses
> ➤ an academic library wanting to improve its service to part-time students
> ➤ a library in the commercial sector wanting to address the needs of its main board of directors
> ➤ a library in a medical charity wanting to provide services to the media.

I hope this short book will convince you to use marketing in your library to benefit your customers, your staff, and your career. Now let's make a start.

Acknowledgments

I would like to extend warm thanks to everyone who put up with me whilst this book was written – my wife and daughter, three creative cats, clients and consultancy colleagues. My appreciation of their encouragement and patience was felt but seldom expressed. Thanks to Helen and Lin at the LA, and to Sheila – I have learnt much from you all. And finally, a message for Graham – thanks for giving me the chance to work with libraries all those years ago. See what happens when you stick your neck out!

Part 1
Making a start in marketing

Introduction to Part 1

If you have ever discussed the marketing of libraries with colleagues you will probably have met the person who says dismissively, 'Oh, we've tried marketing and it doesn't work.'

Unfortunately, if that person happens to be your manager, or their manager, or a person commanding your professional respect and admiration in all LIS matters, this comment can have a demotivating effect on your efforts to improve the marketing of your own library.

Please, before accepting this statement as a wholly accurate and objective summary of this person's experience, dig a little deeper and find out what they mean by marketing.

Many organizations who have tried marketing and found that 'it doesn't work' have not in fact tried marketing at all. They may have placed adverts, sent out press releases, and mailed vast quantities of their latest expensively produced newsletter, but this isn't the whole marketing process.

This error is not exclusive to libraries - many commercial organizations make the same mistake, confusing these activities with the complete process of marketing. I believe this misconception is largely caused by the fact that the proper label for this part of the marketing process is the 8-syllable term 'marketing communications' which is naturally shortened to the 3-syllable term 'marketing' at every opportunity.

Part One explains the complete process of marketing, the steps involved, and the role of each one. It stresses the importance of establishing who your customers really are, and what you want to tell them, before attempting to communicate with them.

By the end of Part One you should have a better understanding of your customers, the marketplace in which you operate, and your own organization. You will also be able to explain to your customers, managers, funders and staff why you do what you do and why they should support your efforts.

Chapter 1
What is marketing and why should libraries use it?

In this chapter you'll find out:
- ➤ what marketing really is
- ➤ how to relate the principles of classic product marketing to a service
- ➤ how to take your first steps in achieving a marketing strategy of your own.

The objections to marketing

Marketing is an activity that is easy to put off till another day. Do you recognize this reluctant library manager, who can always justify avoiding the marketing of their library?

> The trouble is, there's not enough time to even think about this at the moment, and you know we don't have any money to spend. If it doesn't work there will be hell to pay with senior management. And if it does work, how will we cope with all the additional work? And if we start asking what the customers really want, won't that just show up all our weaknesses? And anyway, we're always busy so we must have enough customers, so we must be doing the right things already. What good could marketing possibly do?

These points will be discussed at the end of the chapter, but for now let's discuss what marketing really is and how it can help you serve your customers.

Marketing is . . .

Marketing is the application of some common sense to the business of providing a product or service for your customers. Note the use of the term 'for customers'. 'For' is used because your services are not provided 'to' anyone – this implies the absence of a need for that product. Providing services 'for' customers focuses on their requirements, enabling you to fulfil their needs. And the term 'customer' is used because only computers and drug dealers have users. Everyone else, including libraries, have customers.

Exercise

Before explaining the process of marketing, it would be useful if you put the book down for just two or three minutes to consider what the word 'marketing' means to you. Write down three or four words that you associate with the term.

Hands up all those who came up with words like 'advertising', 'selling', and 'cost'. Well done: these are satisfactory responses – advertising is sometimes used in marketing campaigns, selling is nearly always needed to persuade people to 'buy' your products and services, and marketing isn't always free, so yes, a cost is involved.

If you responded with words like 'customer', 'planning' or 'investment', then go to the top of the class right now and pat yourself on the back. You already appreciate that marketing is not about you, it's about

---

Think . . .

What value do you bring to your customers' lives? How do they use the knowledge and information they acquire from you? How would they be affected if you couldn't help them? Can they go somewhere else? Would they go without? What are the effects of this?

From the millions of people all over the world who COULD benefit from your service, who would benefit the most and are they the ones that currently come to you for help? What specific products or services do you offer to make their lives easier? What expectations do your customers have? How are you meeting them? How are you failing to meet them? Are these expectations realistic? Can they be changed?

These people who should be using your library, do they know about you? If not, why not? If they do know of you, what do they know about you? Are they right?

---

your customers, that your approaches to the people you choose to call customers must be planned, and that reaching the right customer is an investment in the future, not an operational cost.

So, what is marketing?

Marketing requires that you focus on what you do, why you do it, who you do it for, and how you do it. If you want to be successful you must know these things, either by instinct, or by planning.

Successful organizations constantly ask these difficult questions and use the answers to move forward, to build on their strengths and to improve on their weaknesses. They are using the process of marketing, which provides a set of tools to help them focus on their customers' needs – they conduct market research, write mission statements, perform marketing audits, segment their market and produce marketing plans. They use these tools to define their marketing strategy.

When they communicate with customers they use other tools – more market research, promotional literature, advertising, public relations, newsletters, seminars, direct mail, exhibitions, seminars, special campaigns, websites. These are the tools of a marketing communications programme.

If this is starting to sound a bit theoretical, like your last management seminar that gave you good ideas but no pointers on how to make them work, don't despair! Marketing is really very simple; in fact I'll describe the whole process in just six words. Here goes . . .

➤ Marketing anticipates and meets customer demand.

Marketing is NOT . . .

There are a number of harmful myths about marketing so let's dispel some of them before we go any further.

Marketing is not selling

Marketing starts with customers and selling starts with product or service.

➤ Marketing identifies your customers needs, then plans to fulfil them.

➤Selling starts with the products you have and aims them at your customers.

The famous management guru Peter Drucker maintained that the aim of marketing is to make selling unnecessary. This laudable aim is not always possible – even the smartest marketing operation sometimes needs a little help. But no amount of persuasion will attract customers to an organization that does not understand their needs – and that is where marketing pays off.

➤Marketing is getting on your customers' shortlist – preferably a shortlist of one!
➤Selling is persuading customers that you are the best organization for the job. If you are a fisherman, marketing reels them in and selling lands them in the net.

By focusing on the customer, marketing identifies your *raison d'être* – after all, without customers you have no reason to exist.

Marketing is not advertising

Advertising is one of the media that can be used to promote products and services to selected customers. It is one of many methods of communicating with the market and it will be more fully discussed in Chapter 5. Advertising is not always the best way to communicate with customers but marketing is the only way that will help you make that decision.

Marketing is not just for the marketing department

Although few libraries have their own marketing staff, it is the job of everyone to consider what they do from the customer's perspective and to help the organization adapt to the needs of those whom you exist to serve. Everyone.

Marketing is not about making money (unless you want it to)

Whether your library is part of a profit-making organization or a public or welfare body, successful marketing must support the overall objectives of your organization. If it makes sense for your library to make a profit by charging some categories of customer for some services, then marketing will help do this. If, on the other hand, your service is dedicated to providing services completely free of charge to everyone wishing to use it, then marketing will help achieve this too.

Marketing is not just for organizations that sell products

Although the classic four 'P's of marketing (product, price, place and promotion) were conceived with products in mind, they can also be used for services. Although there is no compulsion to use the four 'P's in your marketing analysis, they are so often used as an excuse not to entertain 'proper' marketing of services that it is useful to show how they can be applied in the marketing of library services.

P is for product

The right *product* that is designed to meet the customer's needs can just as easily be the right service. Sometimes, giving a service a 'product' name helps brand the service, creating an identity in the mind of the customer and positioning it in the marketplace against other places they could go for their information.

Products are tangible, having a physical presence that can be held, or touched, or demonstrated. Libraries use products like books, journals and CD-ROMs to deliver their service and these products can be used to promote the library in a number of ways. They can be physically 'demonstrated' at open days or evenings, seminars, induction courses and teach-ins, and at the launch of new services. Their effective use can be demonstrated in case studies, articles for the press and personal networking.

You can also demonstrate the added value you provide for customers by showing:

➤ how your knowledge of information resources and subject expertise can enhance their search for information
➤ how you help identify and specify their needs more accurately and cogently

9

➤ how recognition of their objectives helps you provide 'better', more useful information

➤ how you make a direct contribution to the achievement of their objectives.

This is the added value you bring to your customers.

Exercise

Cast your mind back over the last two weeks or so and identify three customers your library has helped by adding value to their request. List them and add the names of other customers, or types of customer, that would benefit from the added value you provide.

Each service transaction – each time your customer comes to you for answers and solutions – is unique in time and place. The same individual will use your service many times with different needs each time. Seemingly identical queries from different customers will be resolved using different techniques and varied sources.

Customers often identify the providers of a service with the service itself. This does not happen with products. For your library service the quality of the transaction itself – the experience of asking for and receiving information – will often determine whether a customer returns.

Far from being a problem, this is an opportunity. Your professionalism, expertise, integrity, communication and interpersonal skills, even your cheerfulness and friendly disposition, add to the value of your service. Although these attributes are not by themselves enough to guarantee success, customers are more likely to return if they enjoy the service transaction, and this is a factor under your direct control.

In short, there are not many products as flexible as the unique, one-off, intangible information service that serves as your product.

P is for price

The right *price* relates to service as much as it does to any product. Where charges are made they will usually need to cover costs, be competitive with other suppliers, be affordable to your customers and reflect the value of your service in meeting their particular needs.

P is for place

Marketing models for products dictate that they should be available to customers wherever the customers want them. For example, the right 'place' for confectionery products used to be specialist retail outlets. Now you can buy them almost anywhere – petrol stations, cinemas, grocery stores, even chemists.

The right *place* shows your library at its best. Your customers have access to your service at any time of day, from any place in the world, if you choose to give it to them. They can visit in person, by telephone, fax, or e-mail, using the postal system, or by browsing your website. You want the right place ? You've got it !

P is for promotion

The right *promotion* is what much of this book is about. Communicating with your customers and potential customers using various media, conveying the images and text that best describe how you can meet their needs, is just as vital for a service provider as for the company selling products. Some of the choices may be different – few library managers will need to enquire about television advertising rates while Coca-Cola is unlikely to invite you to an open evening, but the principles are the same.

How might these four 'P's be used in our case study libraries?

The public library, with particular reference to business information

Product
➤ books for loan on general management and specific disciplines, e.g. accountancy, human resources, sales and marketing
➤interlibrary loans for items not held at this library
➤a wide variety of business and industry-specific journals
➤national newspapers in print and CD-ROMs
➤reference material (print and CD-ROM) on specific industries and markets (directories, yearbooks, etc.)
➤business news on CD-ROM

Continued

➤company annual reports
➤Companies House information
➤patent information
➤material from local business clubs and agencies
➤expertise on use of the Internet for business information.

Price
Many services are free of charge: loans, enquiries, use of books, journals, and CD-ROMs. Charges are made for company searches, patent searches, use of and printing from the Internet, printing from CD-ROMs, interlibrary loans and photocopying.

Place
In current order of popularity:

1. Personal visit, during normal opening hours
2. Telephone and fax enquiries
3. Some businesses have asked if the library can put information on a library website, and answer queries by e-mail. This is being costed.

Promotion
As later chapters will show, the following methods will be important:
➤public relations (PR)
➤advertising
➤direct mail
➤exhibitions.

The academic library, with particular reference to part-time students

Product
➤loans of subject-specific books and study aids, including 'how to study' material
➤interlibrary loans
➤subject-specific journals
➤library pages on the college website
➤reference material including CD-ROMs and use of the Internet
➤training on the use of these reference tools.

Continued

Price
➤All services are provided free of charge to registered students.

Place
➤in person, mostly during evening opening hours
➤the library website and e-mail, especially by students on placement
➤telephone and fax enquiries.

Promotion
As later chapters will show, the following methods will be important:

➤relationships with tutors
➤advertising
➤direct mail
➤enrolment days.

Industrial/commercial library, with particular reference to the Board of Directors

Product
➤ loan of books and reports on general management, specific disciplines, and specific industries, subjects, companies and markets
➤ a wide variety of national and international journals, some circulated to key individuals
➤ abstracting of articles in key journals
➤ online databases carrying technical, financial, market and industrial news
➤ national and international newspapers in print and on CD-ROM
➤ official publications from national government, the European Union and various international agencies
➤ knowledge of quality websites
➤ library pages on the company intranet
➤ comprehensive collection of company annual reports
➤ interlibrary loans
➤ general reference material including CD-ROMS
➤ current awareness bulletins by subject
➤ selective dissemination of information (SDI) to individuals on a project basis.

Continued

Price
Library costs are currently met from the cross-charging of departments for central services; a plan to charge hourly rates for research work is being considered.

Place
➤ company intranet
➤ e-mail enquiries
➤ telephone and fax enquiries
➤ personal visit.

Promotion
As later chapters will show, the following methods will be important:

➤ advertising
➤ direct mail
➤ presentations.

Medical charity library, with particular reference to the media

Product
➤ subject specific and general health books and journals
➤ medical online databases
➤ reference and enquiry service
➤ knowledge of quality websites in the field
➤ library pages on the charity website
➤ current awareness bulletin/newsletter.

Price
Currently free of charge but new services for the media may be charged.

Place
➤ telephone and fax enquiries
➤ e-mail enquiries and use of website.

Promotion
As later chapters will show, the following methods will be important:

➤ PR
➤ advertising
➤ direct mail.

Your marketing plan

The starting point for any marketing activity must be the marketing plan. I know you've heard this before and that the thought of yet another plan doesn't thrill you, but this one will be really worthwhile. This plan is the fundamental step in the marketing process and one that is often missed out.

Your plan need not be long or complex. It might fill several pages but it might require only a page or two. Remember, it's not the size that matters but the quality! The more honest you can be about your own library (which is not as easy as it sounds) and the more searching the questions you ask yourself (and your customers), the more useful the plan will be.

The plan itself is less important than the knowledge you gain by seeking answers to the following questions, although the act of writing it down is in itself a first commitment to implementation. How many unwritten plans have you carried out lately?

> ## Think . . .
> ➤ What are your aims and objectives?
> ➤ Which of these are you currently meeting, and how?
> ➤ Assuming you are not currently meeting all your objectives, how do you propose to do so?

Remember, the successful plan is not necessarily the most accurate, best written or the best presented. It is the one that is implemented. This does not mean you can throw it together without careful thought and execution – accuracy and honesty are important and well presented plans will increase your chance of success. But any plan is ultimately useless if it is not turned into action.

An imperfect plan implemented well is far preferable to a 'perfect' plan that is left on the shelf. To ensure the plan is implemented you should seek the advice and support of staff at all levels in your organization. Use all your contacts and develop new ones to ensure you get the backing you need.

Let's look at the questions posed by your marketing plan in more detail.

What are your aims and objectives?

The succinct answer to this question is in your mission statement. Unfortunately, so many organizations have mission statements that are vacuous – either too long or unintelligible (or both) – that the term has fallen into disrepute. Asking you to construct one for your library is unlikely to be met with much enthusiasm so I am going to suggest that you write a positioning statement, or a statement of purpose, instead.

This is a cunning way of getting you to write a sentence or two that answers three questions summarizing what you do and why. The questions are :

➤ what type of customer uses (or should use) your library?
➤ what do you do for those customers?
➤ how do you do it?

Exercise

Do this now for your own library. Look at the examples below and write two or three sentences that together form a statement that answers the question 'What are you here for?'

A small public library might have the following positioning statement: 'Towntees Branch Library serves the resident and working population of the Borough of Towntees by providing for all their information needs and recreational reading requirements, answering queries and making available its large stock of fiction and non-fiction books, as well as CD-ROMs and records/cassette tapes.'

Or a positioning statement for the information centre in a plc company might read: 'The Information Centre of Ridgmount plc meets the information needs of all employees (worldwide) by providing access to its hard copy and electronic information resources with the help of library staff with specialist knowledge and by facilitating direct access.'

After you have spent between 10 and 30 minutes on this exercise (don't take longer than this at the moment) you should realize that these statements are not always easy to write but they do help you focus on the fundamentals of your library by producing a clear statement of what you are about.

If you completed this exercise then you now have a positioning statement for your library and are well on your way to describing your aims and objectives. Chapter 2 will discuss how you can use this statement to segment your market, defining the needs of your different market sectors with more precision.

Armed with the knowledge of what each of your different markets want, you will be able to specify the objectives of your library. Which of these demands, sometimes excessive, sometimes conflicting, do you aim to fulfil? When this is completed you will be able to evaluate your services and design new ones, determining the priorities and resources required for each one.

Which of your objectives are currently being met, and how?

This question requires brutal honesty about your service to customers. Whether or not you have already started to ask them for their views on your current performance and what new services they would like, now is the time to ask more searching questions.

Think . . .

Are you meeting their objectives when they come to your library? How and why are you meeting them? Is it because there is nowhere else to go for this service? Or is it because your library provides a better, quicker or cheaper service?

If you are not meeting their needs, why not? Are you too expensive, in the wrong location, inaccessible in some way, short of resources, short of staff, unknown to the customers, or does the competition offer such a good service that you are not even considered?

If your service is under-used investigate the reasons why. There may be sound reasons for improving it but if necessary do not be afraid to admit that it is no longer relevant to customers' needs.

Continued

Who are your competitors? Are they external organizations? Are they profit-making? Are they internal to your organization? What is their strategy for attracting your potential customers? Do they target them aggressively? Which methods of promotion do they use: direct mail, advertising, or public relations? How do they keep in touch with their customers? Do they have a sales force? Or do your customers approach them for help because they do not know about you, or because you have let them down in the past?

Much of this information can be gleaned from examining the press. Make sure you read your customers favourite journals – if only to look at the advertising! For example, if your Board of Directors is an important market sector, make sure you know which of your competitors advertise in the key management journals and look closely at the message they use to promote their service. What is their message to their customers?

Similarly, find out whether they are sending direct mail to your customers and perform the same analysis. What are they sending them and what sales message are they concentrating on? In sales-speak this is their unique selling proposition, or USP. Do their adverts emphasize their range of services, speed of delivery, content, accessibility, price? Remember that USPs are seldom, in fact, unique – if it works for them it could work for you as well.

Contact them and get on their mailing lists. One of the great advantages of being in the information business is that you are often a potential customer as well as a competitor. Use this to your advantage.

Your customers go to you for a number of reasons, some of them not easy to distinguish from each other, but what is the overriding reason that makes a particular customer approach you and not some other organization? The answer is not always obvious.

Think . . .

➤ how many cars have you bought because you liked the sound the door made when it shut?

➤ have you ever bought a house for a reason that was totally illogical or irrational but was so important at the time that all other factors paled into insignificance?

> ## Exercise
>
> What is the USP of your library? Write down as many reasons you can think of for using your library, then rank them according to their importance to the customer (this should only take a few minutes). Now ask a few of your customers what they think. It's best if they have no knowledge of your list so their responses are unprompted. Ask them why they go to you – ask them by telephone, by e-mail, or stop them at random in the library.
>
> Were you surprised by their list? Did you anticipate their answers correctly? The normal answers to these questions are 'Yes' and 'No' respectively. This is extremely useful information and if you've never done anything like this before you may be interested to know that you have just completed your first market research assignment!

Some of your potential customers need information but do not seek it out; this inertia or inaction is a form of competition. It is an alternative course of action that can be taken instead of using your services. Why do these individuals do nothing? Do they know what is available? What deters them from approaching you?

As well as talking to your customers you can perform a SWOT analysis to help describe your current situation. SWOT is an acronym for strengths, weaknesses, opportunities and threats.

The SW part concentrates on your organization – its resources, staff, organizational hierarchy, range and quality of services, access points, pricing policies, specialist skills, reputation with the organization and customers, even your current marketing profile. An analysis of these factors will identify your strengths and your weaknesses. The OT part focuses on the external environment by examining how your library is affected by external factors such as:

> ➤ the success of the national economy or employment levels
> ➤ whether the market for your information is growing or contracting or changing for some market sectors more than others
> ➤ social or demographic changes
> ➤ shortages of key resources (e.g. skills)
> ➤ the success of your organization in its own commercial or non-commercial marketplace

➤ the activities and strategies of your competitors

➤ the effect of new technology on your service.

A SWOT analysis can be performed for your library as a whole, for specific types of customer, and for individual services.

SWOT analysis for a small corporate library

Strengths

➤ good reputation with customers

➤ comprehensive collection of books, journals, CD-ROMs and online databases

➤ experienced and knowledgeable staff

➤ effective cataloguing and OPAC system

➤ Librarian reports to Board Director

Weaknesses

➤ not well known outside current customer base

➤ with just two staff, cannot keep up with demand at busy times, difficult to fit training courses in

➤ not enough PCs in library

➤ access problems – pages not yet ready for intranet, library is in an annexe of the main building, far away from most employees, and the only PC with a CD-ROM drive is in the librarian's office

Opportunities

➤ company intranet will reach most employees

➤ company management interested in knowledge management issues

➤ company performance excellent and resources available for expansion

Threats

➤ parent company management have appointed management consultancy to advise on knowledge management issues

➤ some departments consider their own small collection to be adequate for their needs

➤ no natural successor to experienced librarian

SWOT analysis for the online database service in a small corporate library

Strengths
➤ comprehensive subject coverage
➤ expert staff

Weaknesses
➤ expensive pricing structure
➤ cumbersome administrative process for cross-charging of costs

Opportunities
➤ new databases being added at no extra cost
➤ invaluable for expansion of research analysis skills

Threats
➤ the Internet – most staff do not understand the difference in quality
➤ hosts now selling direct to departments who have little expertise in online searching
➤ pricing is moving away from transaction-based costs, increasing the price for low usage

Exercise

Without any further research spend the next few minutes on a SWOT analysis for your own library. Then prepare one for a specific service.

How do you propose to meet your objectives?

This part of your marketing plan will cover the range of services you intend to offer (including pricing policy and method of delivery), how you intend to promote them, and what actions are required to implement the plan. The promotional aspects are covered in Part Two: Communicating with Customers which covers marketing communications.

Before moving onto the task of dividing your customers into precise market sectors, let's find some answers for that reluctant manager who made an appearance earlier this chapter. The objections raised were as follows:

21

'There's not enough time'

Hmmm. Unless you enjoy crisis management, lack of time for planning is not an acceptable reason for shutting your eyes to the changing needs of your customers. Time spent on marketing is time invested in the future, improving your services, helping you understand your customers. The fact that there is always a crisis around when you need one is no excuse for avoiding an important management function.

'There's no money'

Hmmm. If you can get a budget for *any* activity without showing how the allocation of resources will achieve your objectives, then you are in a strange organization indeed. A marketing plan can be used to help get approval for many other plans. In the early days of your marketing effort it's not money you need, it's commitment and time.

'It might not work'

Hmmm. Plans don't work. Ever. Not first-time plans anyway. If they did, everybody would use them. They identify aims, propose courses of action and establish standards to measure the results. They enable you to pinpoint deviation from the desired result and good plans allow for their own modification so the process can be repeated. If you don't want to plan a strategy because it might not work first time, then you are looking for guaranteed success. You're in the wrong job.

'It might work'

Hmmm. This is a tough one. Have you really thought about what this means? You probably think you mean that you're busy enough already and why encourage more customers when you're struggling to cope with the ones you have? Marketing will either confirm that you address your customers needs perfectly all the time (!), or identify areas for improvement. In either case it will help you improve services in a rapidly changing environment.

'It will only show up our weaknesses'

Hmmm. Yes, it will. And if you don't discover them this way maybe you would rather they were pointed out by your customers ? You can run, but you can't hide.

'We're busy so we must be doing the right things'

Hmmm. This is the fallback position of our reluctant manager who feels safe and comfortable in his environment, convinced that it will stay the same for the foreseeable future. If you really think you can escape the consequences of change by pretending it's not going to happen, you are in that famous Egyptian river, denial – deep down, you already know this because your service is almost certainly different to the one you provided a year ago. With or without marketing, change is forced on you.

In short, by anticipating customer needs and pro-actively planning to meet changing demands, marketing enables you to keep pace, sometimes even control, this change.

Summary

➤ There's no point in reading this book if you don't try some hands-on marketing for yourself
➤ Marketing anticipates and meets customer demand
➤ Writing the plan is only the first step: now go and put it into action.

Chapter 2
Who are your potential customers?

> **In this chapter you'll find out:**
>
> ➤ the meaning of 'market segmentation'
> ➤ why it is useful and how it can help you
> ➤ how to segment your market.

Introduction

When you examine your marketplace and try to put a figure on the number of potential customers you have, it will probably be a surprisingly large one. It will include customers of many types, each with different needs and problems, each requiring a slightly different type of service, or a different approach, to make them feel special.

Planning and marketing the different services required by each different type of customer would be an impossible task if you perceived your customer base as one large homogeneous group of individuals with just one shared characteristic – their need for your library services. Fortunately they share other traits and the process of identifying these in order to segment your market is called market segmentation.

What is market segmentation?

Market segmentation is the breaking down of large lists of customers and potential customers into smaller groups (or segments) with shared characteristics in order to provide services closely tailored to fit their needs and expectations. This also allows you to target those customers most likely to be interested in a specific marketing communication.

The following example shows the approach taken by our four case study libraries in segmenting their market. The specific market sector used throughout this book is printed in *bold italics*.

Market segmentation for case study libraries

Public library
➤ Children, segmented into early readers, teenagers and young adults. Further segmentation into literacy, recreational reading, homework, hobbies and GCSE assignments
➤ Adults, segmented into fiction and non-fiction. Fiction further segmented into different genre (crime, horror, sci-fi, fantasy, romance, historical, humour, etc), specific authors, and poetry. Non-fiction further segmented into hobbies, personal interests, domestic or household information (home medicine, DIY etc), and *information for business* or professional use

Academic library
➤ Staff, segmented into teaching staff (then into subject or faculty), management, and other staff.
➤ Students, segmented into full-time and *part-time*, then into subject/faculty and course level ('A' Levels, vocational, undergraduate, postgraduate, etc).

Industrial/commercial library
➤ Main site staff, segmented by department and seniority, including the major departments (Finance, Legal, Human Relations, Sales & Marketing), and the *Board of Directors*.
➤ Staff in UK branches, segmented by geographical area and by job function (middle management, administrative, sales).
➤ Staff in Europe, segmented by language, products sold and subject interest.
➤ Staff outside Europe, segmented by world region, language and access to CD-ROM and Internet/intranet/email technology.

Medical charity library
➤ *Media*, segmented into print (newspapers – international, national, regional, local, and magazines – trade and consumer), television (terrestrial, satellite and cable), and radio (international and UK).
➤ Staff, segmented into office and field staff, by research or operational nature of their job, and by narrow subject interest.
➤ Students, segmented into school and further education.
➤ Medical practitioners, segmented into doctors (GPs, junior doctors and consultants), nurses, teachers, and ancillary professions (counsellors, occupational therapists, physiotherapists, etc.)

Some shared characteristics

➤ age
➤ location
➤ frequency of use
➤ day and/or time of use
➤ ability (or willingness) to pay
➤ job function or status
➤ subject interest
➤ information delivery mechanism
➤ specific needs or problems
➤ critical success factors.

Age

Your public library will clearly distinguish between services offered to early readers, teenagers, or adults, and will communicate with each of these groups using suitable language and imagery.

Location

Some libraries' customers are local to a specific geographical area but others offer a service to a worldwide customer base. A scientific or technical library operating for the benefit of all employees of a company will offer different services for customers on the same company site, those in other parts of the UK, those within Europe, or those within the USA.

Frequency of use

You may choose to offer specific benefits to regular customers or inducements to less frequent and non-customers to use the service.

Day and/or time of use

Some customers will share the characteristic of only being able to use your services at particular times of the day or week. For example, part-time students may only use the library on the days or evenings when their course runs.

Ability (or willingness) to pay

If you are raising income or recovering costs by charging for services then this is a crucial characteristic to identify. There is little point in a business information library targeting its premium (most expensive) service at sole traders and very small companies who may be unwilling, or unable, to pay for it.

Job function or status

Some services will be aimed at individuals performing specific functions or carrying special status. The library within a company might well offer different levels of service to senior managers, and products aimed at individuals performing particular functions or jobs (e.g., researchers, policy advisers, product managers).

Subject interest

A university library will have customers interested only in items relating to their own subject area which may be very narrow or wide. This is also the case in public libraries for both non-fiction and fiction, where the customer's interest may be in a particular author or fiction genre. Specialist libraries, with expertise on a particular industry or technology, will also have customers with a particular subject interest.

Information delivery mechanism

Some customers will only have face-to-face contact with the library and some will only make remote enquiries via the telephone, fax or e-mail. This shared characteristic may not be enough by itself to justify special treatment but it will affect the services offered and the way you communicate with these customers.

Specific needs and problems

Remember that customers tend not to think in terms of 'having needs' at all. When you are in search of information yourself, do you think of your task as a need, or as one facet of a problem you have to solve?

When different customers have the same or similar problems to solve, then that becomes a shared characteristic. Teenagers without access to a school library needing information in order to complete assignments share their problem with adult distance learners with the same need.

Critical success factors (CSFs)

CSFs are something you will read about in marketing books. They are what they say they are – factors critical to your customers' success, often because they are measured against these factors.

For example, if the business analysts within your company need particular financial information by the 25th of every month so it can be included in monthly reports due in on the 1st of every month, then you can make a significant contribution to their success by making sure they receive this information at the right time and in the right format.

> You want the penguin population statistics for Greenland? On the first of every month? On a floppy disc? In the file format of your favourite spreadsheet? With graphs? So you can import them into your own spreadsheet without re-keying? You've got it!

Identifying the factors that are critical to their success has helped you understand their information needs, and making this direct contribution will increase your profile and image with this group of customers and they will become advocates of your library, and probably loyal users of a wide range of services.

Exercise

Choose one of your main customer markets and research their CSFs, their needs and their problems. From this group, choose at least one individual you can approach for more information. Invite them to a semi-working lunch or any other informal setting where social chit-chat can be mixed with a heart-to-heart on those everyday problems they wish they could solve.

At the meeting, avoid specific references to library services, even if they are relevant to the conversation. The object of the exercise is to get them talking about their problems and the ways in which they are being measured or monitored, not about the library.

Continued

After the meeting, record everything you learned and think how the library can *make a contribution* to their future success. Send them a letter, fax, or e-mail within a few days, for example:

'I've been thinking about our conversation last Thursday and wondered if I could help you with the little matter regarding the Chief Accountant's financial ratios. There are CD-ROMs in the library that allow you to select a group of companies and produce all sorts of comparative figures and graphs. It will save you some time and make your reports really stand out. Would you like to talk again about this?'

They will reply in one of three ways. No, you misunderstand me, they *will reply*, even if you have to politely chase them up a little:

➤ positively – 'Great idea, thanks awfully.' This is your cue to add this benefit into your marketing promotions, maybe for a whole market sector – see later chapters.
➤ negatively – 'Why on earth would this help me? What I need is . . .', allowing you to research their needs further.
➤ in a non-committal way – 'Yes, but . . . .' continue until you find out what you can do for them.

Yes, this is a contrived example, and I'm not pretending it will be quite so simple and pain-free as this, but it can produce real benefits. If it doesn't work first time, try again, or change the exercise to fit your own circumstances.

By getting you close to just one or two customers, this exercise should encourage you to focus on ways to contribute to your customers' success in all your market sectors, establishing a two-way communication that will help set your agenda now and in the future.

The benefits of market segmentation

Why should you spend time identifying your different types of customers? What do you get out of it?

➤ it helps you focus on the customers' needs and problems instead of the management issues of providing and maintaining the library.

➤ it helps identify what your customers really need (as well as what they want).You already have a well informed impression of your customers' needs but it is well worth making the effort to re-appraise them, avoiding the preconceptions that exist on both sides of the LIS counter.

➤ you can estimate the size of your market segments. It is often difficult to measure the size of your total market, but by dividing the task into bite sized segments you can get some reasonably accurate and useful figures.

➤ with detailed and specific knowledge of each market sector, you can use messages that really hit the right buttons, highlighting benefits that will make a real difference to customers' lives, instead of relying on one catch-all phrase, or one brochure.

Identifying non-customers

Libraries in a more closed environment, like special libraries, can often identify their customers more easily because there are large groups of people who are denied access to their library. This helps define the customers they *are* expected to serve.

Most libraries have potential customers turned away or referred to a more appropriate agency from time to time, and identifying them can help identify your real customers.

Exercise

Name at least one group of people who regularly ask for information but are clearly NOT your customers: for example, students persistently asking for information and advice from a company library, or an inventor wanting to use their local university library.

Estimate how much time you spend on this group, answering initial queries, explaining why you cannot help them further or referring them to different agencies. Discuss this estimate with at least one other person who is involved in turning them away.

How could you use the time spent on this group? If you only saved half these hours every month, what would you do with them?

In many libraries there is a special category of non-users – people with a major influence over your funding. Even if they are not direct consumers of your products they should be identified as one of your most important market sectors. However important it is to provide an excellent service, it is arguably more important that your funders know just how great a job you are doing.

Exercise

Write down the name of one person closely involved with the funding of your library. You need a name – 'the Chairman of the Library Committee', 'the Director of Research Policy', or the 'Vice-Chancellor' is not enough. These job titles may well decide your future but it is the people that make the decisions. As well as their basic details (name, address, contact details), find out their professional responsibilities and personal interests and whether they use your library (and if so, which services).

Identify at least one item (book, CD-ROM, video, anything the library would or could put to good use) in one of their fields of interest, and ask them to review it because you are considering acquiring it for the library and would like their advice. If this happens to be true, so much the better, but is not essential. Use any response from them as encouragement to build a relationship, and use it to gain a greater understanding of the funding situation, and especially of factors that might help you in the future.

Try not to be put off by the protracted timescale of this exercise – the information gathering should be easy but you may have to wait a considerable time before personal contact can be made. After all, influencers are busy people. If you get no response, make sure your information was correct and either repeat the process or change the target. Over the next few weeks, do this for a few more funding influencers. I think you will be surprised by how much you learn from this exercise. As Woody Allen (allegedly) said:

'80 percent of success is showing up!'

Hints on segmenting your market

Although there are no set rules for segmenting your market the following hints will help you make a start.

> ➤ Every group of customers should be identified, no matter how small. Do not mistake size for importance. You may serve 5000 students, 300 teaching staff and 12 management staff, and you may need to spend a proportionate amount of time on each, but the relative importance of each of these markets is not necessarily related to their size.

> ➤ Remember that individuals can often belong to more than one market segment. At my local public library I am a recreational reader, small businessman, distance learner and the parent of a teenage member of the library, not to mention an author seeking verification of facts and figures (and a place to hide).

> ➤ There is no set number of segments in your market and no minimum size of segment. If just one individual has sufficiently unique needs, and if he or she is different enough or important enough to justify having all their idiosyncrasies satisfied, then you have a market segment consisting of just one person. The logical extension of this argument is that every customer has specific needs, so every customer is a market segment all by themselves; but it is obviously not practical or economic to apply this principle. However, the approach offers lessons for customer care – if you treat everyone *as if* you were there for their sole benefit, you will soon have some very satisfied customers!

➤Apply your information skills to the problem of identifying customer needs. As a library professional, when asked a simple question, what do you do? Answer it? Not immediately, surely? If you've read *Success at the enquiry desk* by Tim Owen in this series (Library Association Publishing, 2nd revised edition, 1998) you make sure you really understand the question, avoid misunderstandings, establish the objectives of the inquirer and agree the task in hand. You should apply a similar critical approach when anticipating the needs of a particular group of customers – you cannot forecast all their future requirements precisely, but a knowledge of the way they work and how they use the information you supply will help you understand what they need from you.

Summary

➤ Market segmentation is breaking your total market into segments
➤ Some non-customers are important too
➤ Satisfying your customers' needs is not enough: you must help them solve their problems
➤ Your success depends on your customers' success.

Chapter 3
What do you want to say, and how do you want to say it?

In this chapter you'll find out:

➤ how to decide what you really want to say
➤ some tips on how to express yourself
➤ your 'power' words and your 'never' words.

Now you know who your customers are and what they need, you are ready to start planning what you want to say to them, to ensure that your library is at the top of their shortlist when they are looking for information and related services.

The right message

Communicating with your market requires that you reach the right audience with the right message in the right way:

➤ the right **audience** – if you're still not sure who your customers are (or should be), then it's back to Chapter 2
➤ the right **message** – this chapter will point you in the right direction
➤ the right **way** – Part Two will discuss the different media available to you and give some hints on how to make best use of them.

What are your objectives?

Given that you now realize your objectives determine your message, what are they? Have you written them down yet? As the following examples show, you are likely to have different objectives for the various market sectors you have identified.

Case study 1: Public library targeting local small businesses

Initial market research suggests that small businesses do not even consider the local library as a source of business information. Their first choice for advice would be their bank manager or accountant, and many assume that the information they require is simply not available so they do not actively seek it out.

The marketing objective for the library is to raise awareness amongst local business, banks, firms of accountants and other business-related agencies. This can be achieved by basing marketing activities on a small number of topical issues of interest to a wide range of the local business community, such as:

➤ the anticipation and management of bad debts and/or late payers
➤ advice for first-time exporters
➤ government and EU funding for research and development of new products.

Specific messages will convey the wide range and affordability of specific information sources, such as company information, market research studies, British standards, trade journals, statistics, government publications, online databases and the Internet. Examples from real life (client profiles or case studies) will show the potential benefits for small businesses and all marketing will stress that the library is:

➤ impartial
➤ easily accessible (location, car parking, opening hours outside normal office hours)
➤ staffed by local people who are highly skilled information professionals.

Case study 2: Academic library targeting part-time students

Very few part-time students use the library, despite the extension of opening hours into the evenings and Saturday mornings. Those that do become regular users and derive much benefit from it. These students express the wish that they had found it sooner.

The marketing objective for the library is to build relationships with full-time staff teaching evening and weekend courses, and with part-time (often freelance) teachers by satisfying special needs and by making sure everyone is included in normal induction activities.

Specific messages will point out that part-time students' course fees include free access to all facilities including the library, as well as highlighting specific services likely to be of interest (for example, inter library loans for items not normally held in stock, or free Internet access) and will stress:

➤ how the library can be of particular help to students returning to study after a long lapse from full-time education
➤ that students with little previous experience of libraries can often get the most benefit from access to new information, leading to improved grades and greater satisfaction with the course and the college
➤ that an enriched learning experience often results in students enroling on further courses.

Case study 3: Industrial/commercial library targeting the Board of Directors

Although information from the library often reaches the Directors it often arrives via intermediaries such as middle or senior management and their Personal Assistants – sometimes they are completely unaware of the library's involvement.

The marketing objective for the library is to position itself versus its competitors for this market:

➤ to identify the source of the directors' information (the company, bankers and accountants, Institute of Directors, regional branch of the CBI, the local Chamber of Commerce etc.)
➤ to provide an in-house service that is faster and more focused towards the objectives of the business than the competition
➤ to emphasize the critical role of the library within the company.

Continued

Specific messages will highlight the comprehensive nature of the facilities available, stressing:

➤ speed of service – simple questions are answered in minutes, and more detailed enquiries within hours
➤ cost – free if it is already covered by management charges
➤ the industry knowledge and expertise of professional staff with a unique blend of information skills and business acumen
➤ confidentiality – when dealing with information of strategic importance there is a commercial advantage in keeping the need for specific data within the company.

Case study 4: Medical charity library targeting the media

Journalists and researchers from the press, television and radio are an important market because they play a vital role in carrying the charity's messages to the public at large and they often use the library to check facts and seek advice. With limited staff numbers this can be very time-consuming, especially when a particular incident prompts all the media to contact the library at the same time.

The marketing objective for the library is to show commitment to this market sector whilst managing demand by providing more information pro-actively and by using a wide range of delivery methods including fax, e-mail and Internet pages.

Specific messages will encourage the media to:

➤ register with the library to receive regular updates (and to ensure they get information circulated to them as part of the 'Front Page' service whereby information is sent out on a pro-active basis when current events create a specific information need)
➤ consult the library Web pages, in particular the frequently asked questions (FAQ) section for basic information and regularly updated statistics
➤ communicate with the library using dedicated fax numbers and e-mail addresses to guarantee a fast response.

How to say what you really mean

Now you know what you want to say to each of your markets, but how do you say it? What are your specific messages, how do you write them down? How do you express them in such a way that every reader cannot fail to be persuaded?

Although you will be producing different types of written material for different audiences, while the writing style of a newsletter (for example) may vary from that used for a press release, there are general guidelines.

General guidelines

Following these general guidelines will help you write better and more effective marketing communications:

➤ branding
➤ language
➤ your 'power' words
➤ the 15-second test
➤ what do they do next?
➤ try it out on someone you know.

Branding

Establishing a clear link between a specific logo, or form of words, or picture, and your information service will be very useful. If a potential customer sees any of your marketing communications (letter, fax, brochure, newsletter, direct mail flier, press release, advertisement, display board, Web page) he or she should be able to instantly recognize it as coming from you. This is called branding.

If I picked up your latest newsletter how long would it take me to realize it came from you? If you consider that an answer of under 10 seconds is good, 10–20 seconds is respectable, 20–30 seconds is poor, and more than half a minute leads to amnesia (What newsletter? Who?) this evidence should convince you to make sure you brand your marketing communications.

If you think this reaction time is over-stated, consider the length of time you take to identify products or services in your domestic and professional life. When you receive mailers, or mailshots, through your front door at home for two different brands of washing powder, my guess is that you can tell the difference between them instantly – in about one second. And I would be surprised if it took you longer than five seconds to identify mailers from different suppliers of similar business products – for example library automation systems, online providers, or library furniture.

Whatever you choose to establish your brand image (the university crest, your favourite slogan, a clipart image) make sure you put it on everything the customer sees. In addition to the high-profile examples listed above, do not forget the less obvious ones. Do you sometimes give your customers a business card? Brand it. Do you send items in the post accompanied only by a compliment slip? Brand it.

The words or logo that are used to represent your brand should be as identical as possible (given any limitations imposed by particular media) on all communications – use the same typeface, capitalization, positioning, and colour. You can and should vary the type size but keeping the same proportions and scale is recommended.

Language

There is a lot of general advice on the subject of copywriting, some of it available in the items listed in the further reading section at the end of this book, and it is all useful and mostly common sense.

This doesn't mean there are rules you can follow which will guarantee success but the advice given points you in the right direction and helps you find the best language for your own environment.

The oft-repeated 'KISS' – Keep it *S*hort and *S*imple – is easy to remember, and good advice. Simple, direct language conveys information quicker and better than copy that may be more grammatically correct and long-winded.

As far as possible use unambiguous words and everyday vocabulary; if there is a particular reason why you have to use jargon (and I mean 'have to' – do not use it without questioning whether it really is necessary), then give the meaning in a highlighted or shaded box, or include a glossary, or find some way of explaining the term for customers who do not use the term in their everyday language.

Avoid exaggeration and unsubstantiated claims – edit your copy not just for typographic errors but examine carefully every promise made to make sure you are saying what you really mean.

Your 'power' words

Use words that you have already identified as your 'power' words. These are words you think will especially attract your customers (or perhaps just one market sector), creating the right image for your service.

Exercise

Here is a list of power words that are commonly found in marketing communications. They are general in nature and not specific to the LIS field and may include words you hate. They are meant to include derivations – for example, 'special' is meant to include 'specialist and specialize', and 'reliable' includes 'rely'.

In a small group, discuss which of these words (if any) are power words for your library, adding new ones that you feel are appropriate. You should aim to finish with a list of 12–15 words that you can use in marketing communications.

- new
- professional
- reliable
- proven
- free
- safe
- convenient
- effective (or cost-effective)
- special
- flexible
- valuable
- service

If you have time, discuss a list of 'never' words – words you must avoid using at all costs! Then make sure they never appear in anything a customer might see.

The 15-second test

Some forms of communication require this additional check to evaluate whether the reader gets a summary of the whole document in the first few words or sentences.

Exercise

If you have one, give one of your press releases, or a direct mailing letter, to someone who is not completely familiar with your library. Ask them to read it as if they had received it by post – stop them after about 15 seconds. Ask them what they think the document is all about, from what they have read so far.

If they accurately report the main message(s) you wanted to convey then well done!

If not, visualize a busy customer or a frantic editor reading their mail. If the main thrust of the message hasn't hit home in 15 seconds the chance of them reading on to get to the good stuff is severely reduced.

So don't save your best copy for the last paragraph (or even the middle one) – hit them hard with your message right at the start when you have their best attention.

Make it easy to respond

You've written some arresting copy, the document is branded so readers can have no doubt who it comes from, they read the first few sentences and are interested enough to read on, and they want to contact you. Have you told them how?

I know it's a silly question, no-one would ever send out a mailer or brochure without their address, telephone and fax numbers, email and website address, and contact names, would they?

Hands up everyone who has, at one time or another, tried in vain to locate these details on promotional information. Enough said – make sure you don't make this mistake.

Try it out on someone you know

When you have finished writing any marketing communication do these three things:

➤ read it out loud (to yourself)
➤ ask someone who knows your library but not in too much detail to comment on it
➤ pilot the document – send it to a small representative sample of the target readership.

Consider these points as reminders. There will be times when they will be inappropriate – for example, piloting press releases would tend to take the edge off the newsworthiness of the item, so don't do it. But there again, for releases of a more general nature it might still be appropriate, so think about it before deciding.

Summary

➤ **You are aiming to reach the right audience with the right message in the right way (in that order)**
➤ **If in doubt, brand it!**
➤ **Use your power words and avoid your never words**
➤ **Always try before you fly!**

Part 2
Communicating with customers

Introduction to Part 2

Now that you know who your customers are and the messages you want to convey to them, you are ready to communicate with them, or in other words, to use marketing communications.

You will reach out to every potential customer of your library. But how? There is a wide choice of media competing for your limited marketing budget so how do you decide which ones are right for you? They are all useful and the right mix for you can only be achieved by experimentation.

Every marketing medium sends your message in a different way, and each one aims to elicit a response. Several models of this marketing communication process have been proposed – one of the most useful is known by the acronym AIDA, which stands for attention, interest, desire and action.

This model proposes that the objective of any communication is to attract the attention of the customer, gain their interest so they desire your products and service, and take some action towards achieving their desire.

Your objective is therefore to use the qualities of each medium to get your customers' attention, interest and desire, make it easy for them to respond to you, and above all, get some action.

The next four chapters will deal with the following marketing media:

➤ PR (public relations)
➤ advertising
➤ direct mail
➤ exhibitions, roadshows, seminars, etc.

Chapter 4
Public relations

In this chapter you'll find out:

➤ **why every library should be using PR**
➤ **how to choose the right targets for your library**
➤ **how to reach them.**

I have some favourite paradoxes of modern living. My (current) top three are :

➤Why doesn't the word 'phonetic' begin with an 'f' ?
➤Why is there only one Monopolies Commission? and
➤Why does PR get such a bad press?

The very mention of PR brings to mind images of shallow people living off large expense accounts who are interested only in hype. But in reality PR professionals are extremely effective communicators and they have a lot to teach us part-time marketeers.

Definition

Public relations is the planned and sustained communication of your messages to your target markets using the public media of print, broadcast, and electronic press. The primary tool for communicating with these media is the press release but you can also build relationships with the editorial staff of newspapers, magazines, radio and TV programmes by inviting them to events (open evenings, product launches, seminars, etc.) organized with publicity in mind.

PR works because . . .

PR gives more authority and credibility

PR gives more authority and credibility than other forms of promotion like advertising, where readers know that the message is under the direct control of the advertiser and allow for this in their response.

PR promotes your library to the right people

Regular news in the editorial pages of your customers' favourite magazines will be worth thousands of pounds in advertising terms after just a few months, and the cumulative effect of this exposure will make your library easier to recall than other information providers who have not been featured as well or as often.

PR parades your success

As well as providing 'independent' communication with your customers, PR parades your success in front of other important audiences (or publics, as they are called by the Institute of Public Relations). The funders of your library, your partners and suppliers, even major influencers and community leaders, will see items in the press as confirmation of their decision to support you. They can bask in your glory, share your profile, and be reminded just how important their contribution is to your success. That's right, it's covert lobbying.

PR is 'cheaper' than advertising

PR is 'cheaper' than advertising because it requires no large cheques to be signed, giving a rather false impression that it is 'free'. In truth, it requires your commitment, and this is not a cheap commodity. It is also a continuous process – you cannot have a meeting in January and decide what will be newsworthy for each month that year.

Choosing your target markets

In the last two chapters you have set out your specific market sectors and objectives for each one. Now you need to decide which specific message(s) you want to convey using PR as the tool.

Exercise

Select one of your market sectors and write down your objectives for that market. What is it that you want them to know (or better still, understand) after this campaign? This should take less than 15 minutes.

Your target media

You will want your news broadcast in media that are read, listened or viewed by your target audience so you need to find out which media your customers favour. An obvious method is to ask them:

> ➤ 'Which magazines and journals do you read to keep in touch?'
> ➤ 'Which radio stations do you listen to?'
> ➤ 'At what times of day do you listen?'
> ➤ 'For local news, do you favour BBC or ITV?'

You should also take note of where your competitors advertise, or where you see their press releases printed.

From the list of media that emerges from this market research, select a few strategic targets (the media that reach a high proportion of any of your target markets) that can be singled out for special attention. You will need:

> ➤ The names of the publication, the Editor, and other relevant editorial staff, as well as address, telephone, fax and e-mail contact details.
> ➤ The copy dates for each issue or programme. This is the date by which news items must be received if they are to be considered for the next issue, helping to avoid the frustration of discovering your news would have been printed if it had been received a day earlier.

➤The profile of their readers/listeners/viewers. What job titles do they have? Where are they in the country, or in the world? Which industries do they represent? How much money do they spend? What are their particular interests? How old are they?

In short, you want to know everything the publication knows about its own readers to help you identify what they will find newsworthy and write appropriate copy.

This list is less daunting than it looks. The information is already collected to help them sell advertising space. Ask them for a media pack, a sample copy, and to be put on the 'controlled circulation list' which guarantees a free copy of every issue.

For professional and trade magazines the media pack will include a features list for the year. This allows you to predict when you have a better chance of attracting the notice of the Editor. For example, if the April issue features agricultural information, and you have a contribution to make, make contact two months before their copy date to find out what sort of 'story' they are looking for. This will give you a head start over organizations sending unsolicited press releases.

Do not ignore the value of sending your press releases to relevant World Wide Web sites and electronic magazines/journals/newsletters.

Exercise

For the market sector you chose in the last exercise, write down the places they go for professional and/or recreational information – journals, magazines, national and local newspapers, local radio programmes, websites.

Choose three or four publications or programmes, contact each publication, ask for their media pack and to be added to their controlled circulation.

Compare their readership profiles with your own target market to ensure the list matches your requirements.

What is a press release?

A press release is a brief item of news about your library, sent to the Editor of a newspaper, magazine, or even a local radio or TV news programme, so they can include it in their next issue for publication or broadcast.

Press releases have a particular format and Editors will expect:

➤ a clear heading stating that it is a press release, and who it is from
➤ a prominently displayed date
➤ a title – an eye-catching title is a bonus but don't worry if it is merely business-like
➤ double-spaced text
➤ a first paragraph summarizing the whole item, so that the Editor can assess its newsworthiness within a few seconds – normally about 30 words in length
➤ text describing and naming your product or service, who it is aimed at, where it originates (your library), and why your topic is relevant to this set of readers
➤ simple, clear, jargon-free language, avoiding excessive use of superlatives
➤ acronyms to be explained – they might not know that NYR means National Year of Reading
➤ some background text for the editorial staff, not intended to be part of the press release, about your library, including details of any additional material you can supply on request, like photographs of the building or staff
➤ the contact details of your library
➤ a name and contact details for follow up calls from the press, including details of your website if you have one.

PR is about news

Editors are bombarded by unsolicited press releases and your challenge is to make yours stand out from the rest. They must be so newsworthy that they are immediately put in the 'print this' pile on the editor's desk.

Editors are always looking for news – that means your press release must convey news first and information second. You must persuade them that your information is so topical and interesting to their readers that they simply must print it. Remember, no matter how interesting you think your story is, the only viewpoint considered by the Editors is that of their readers.

Make sure the word 'new' is in every press release you write, preferably in the first paragraph. If you are writing about something that is not new, ask yourself why customers need to know about it and try to find a single aspect that is new. For example, if you have sent press releases about your new mobile library for disabled people months ago, but without success, why not invite a local councillor, or your MP, or the Chief Executive of a relevant charity to perform a grand (re-) opening and invite the press to attend?

There are many other ways of injecting 'news' into your PR activity, including:

➤ **Case studies.** A story about the distance learner using their local public library, or relating how a college tutor saved his/herself and his/her students time and effort by working closely with the college library would attract attention and interest. Case studies are attractive to Editors because they know their readers like real-life stories, particularly when they have something in common with the featured individual or organization.

➤ **Articles about suitably topical subjects that publicize your library.** Use your subject knowledge to explain the benefits of (for example) company information in market research, extolling the virtues (subtly, of course) of your own service. Editors are always looking for contributors who can save them time and resources.

➤ **Talks by your management and staff can be publicized through the press.** If someone from your library gives a paper at a conference then make a song and dance about it! Whether it is at the local Round Table or at a prestigious international conference, it provides a good news story for your customers.

➤ **Organize events to raise your profile.** Are there any anniversaries coming up or commemorative events you can get involved in? If the library has a special collection on (say) aerospace, take advantage of the next high profile air show by writing something for a relevant magazine. Can you use your contacts with the local book trade to ensure that the famous author visiting local bookshops to sign their latest epic makes a stop at your library?

➤ **Make sure that an expert in particular subjects is available to provide quotes for journalists.** They might be from the local newspaper or *Ferret Fanciers Weekly* – but if you can get on their list of reliable sources you can get a mention for your library.

Building relationships with your media

Sending out press releases is just the first step in PR – your success will be determined by how many are chosen by editors and others for inclusion in their media.

You can boost the chance of success by building good relationships. Start by discussing your overall aims and objectives with each Editor, and by explaining why your information will be of direct and topical interest to their readers. Later they might even contact you to ask for news items that satisfy their explicit requirements – if they have requested something from you then there is a better chance it will be used.

Exercise

Look at the sample copies you collected in the previous exercise. Do they include short news items, longer articles, or case studies? Is the issue highly focused on the featured topic of the month or does this constitute just one article? What is the copy date for the next issue?

Choose one publication from your list and telephone the Editor. Point out that you are embarking on a campaign to inform his readers about your services and ask their opinion on the best type of information to supply. Be ready to answer lots of questions about your library, in particular why their readers will be interested in it. Make sure you ask about anything unusual in their requirements for the press release itself ('We never consider faxes or e-mails', or 'It should be addressed to the News Editor', etc.).

As a result of this conversation write a short press release (maximum 300 words) on something newsworthy and send it to the Editors of these publications.

Following up

If you follow the advice in this chapter and your press release is newsworthy you have every chance of getting it published or broadcast, but do not despair if it is not used. Editors (or their staff) will normally help you understand why it wasn't chosen. Remember that Editors cannot print everything they would like to, they have difficult choices to make too.

You should keep copies of all press releases, marking those that are published or broadcast so they can be used in other promotions and to show your success to your funders and colleagues.

If you feel that your press releases are genuinely newsworthy and still not being printed, check the medium and the message:

➤ telephone the editors and ask for advice

➤ you might be sending your news to the wrong publications – check the media pack and compare the profile with your customers again to make sure you understand why they read this and what they get from it. If the Editor doesn't think your news is relevant to them there must be a reason: ask them

➤ you might be sending information that is not news – look at your press releases and re-write them using the guidelines above. This should ensure you do better next time.

➤ you might be using an inappropriate style for a particular publication. Although computers make it easy to send the same document to different organizations, sometimes you need to tailor the style of a press release to reflect the requirements of a particular publication or even Editor. Compare your press release with the style in your sample copies.

Exercise

From the press releases sent out for the previous exercise, select those that were not used and telephone the Editor to find out the reasons. Maybe it was for one of the reasons above or perhaps it was purely pressure of space in that particular issue. If so, ask if it will be reconsidered for the next week or month or ask if there are any other items of news they are looking for.

For those that were published, well done! Now build on this by building a larger list and diarizing some time to consider each month's PR opportunities and act upon them.

Finally, how might our case study libraries use PR as a marketing tool?

Case study 1: Targeting local small business

PR is an important tool in the marketing of this service. The media will include:

➤ local business newspapers/magazines published by Chambers of Commerce, branches of the CBI etc., for example *Company Digest* (mailed to Managing Directors and chief executives in Surrey, Hampshire, and East and West Sussex), *North East Hampshire Chamber of Commerce Newsletter*, *Blackwater Bugle* (published by the Blackwater Valley Small Business Club), and *Gateway* (published by Southampton Chamber of Commerce)

➤ local press such as the *Farnborough/Aldershot Mail*, *The Surrey Advertiser*, *The Farnham Herald*, and the free newspapers

➤ local radio news and business programmes (BBC Southern Counties and independent Eagle Radio)

➤ local TV news and business programmes (Meridian TV, BBC South-East).

Regular press releases will be sent on topics like:

➤ new or improved services (e.g. a new patent search service, or reduced prices for Internet access)

➤ new information sources available, especially those relevant to local industries

➤ client profiles, showing how local companies have benefited from access to the library.

Continued

➤ news of seminar programmes (both before and after) raising topical issues like the millennium bug, coping with bad debts and late payment, exporting for beginners and getting grants to fund research and development. Some of these will be organized in conjunction with the local Business Link and other agencies
➤ news of visits to the library by local business groups, and of library staff making presentations and talks to these groups.

Personal contact will be established with Editors wherever possible (but especially with the strategic media – local business press) to help them with their own information needs and to increase awareness of the library's activities, with the objective of getting early notice of PR opportunities.

All targeted publications/programmes will be scanned for information on companies known to be using the library, enabling a wish-list of client profiles to be built. When any customer wins a business award, substantial grant, or prestigious new contract, personal contact will be made to see if they could become involved with some aspect of the library's events (for example, they could host a seminar meeting.)

Case study 2: Academic library targeting part-time students

PR is not considered to be the main marketing tool for building closer relationships with teaching staff because the market is easy to reach using more personal marketing methods. However, the following actions are recommended:

➤ notices and information highlighting the library can be placed in college newsletters and other publications, especially in the list of courses distributed to the public from May till September
➤ in addition to leaflets designed specifically for part-time students, a new section should be added to the library newsletter for this audience, discussing issues relating to their particular needs.

Case study 3: Industrial/commercial library targeting the Board of Directors

PR is not considered to be the main marketing tool for reaching this internal audience as they are a small and well known group of people and easy to reach but there are some activities that can reinforce messages conveyed by more direct marketing tools:

➤ inform the company newspaper of recent acquisitions of topical interest to senior management
➤ the library newsletter will include a new section relating current news (business, political, economic, technological, environmental) to the strategic issues facing the company
➤ ensure the library has prominent pages on the company intranet, and keep it up-to-date and topical.

Case study 4: Medical charity library targeting the media

PR is an important tool in the marketing of this service. The targeted media will include:

➤ national newspapers regularly featuring medical stories (the *Mail*, the *Guardian*, the *Sunday Times* and others)
➤ magazines devoted to family health and medical issues (for example, *Health and fitness* and *Your health*)
➤ newsletters provided by self-help and other voluntary groups
➤ radio and TV news programmes
➤ radio and TV medical programmes
➤ freelance journalists with an interest in medical subjects.

In addition to the charity's PR activity promoting the charity's overall objectives, the library will send their own press releases to tell the media about:

➤ information services available for the media
➤ current developments in the field (e.g. summarizing new findings reported in online databases or reputable websites)
➤ current awareness FAQ (a monthly or quarterly frequently asked questions update to communicate the latest thoughts and fears of sufferers and carers).

Within the charity, library staff will strengthen relationships with other departments, identifying opportunities to promote the role of the library.

Summary

➤ PR is a planned and sustained activity requiring time and effort
➤ Keep a constant look-out for NEWS that can be used to achieve your marketing objectives
➤ Don't be afraid to make some news yourself.

Chapter 5
Advertising

In this chapter you will:

➤ decide whether advertising is for you and your library
➤ consider how advertising is perceived by customers.

Why should libraries consider advertising at all?

Let me guess what you are thinking right now: 'Advertising is expensive. I am given very little money to spend on marketing my library. Therefore, I cannot afford to advertise and why should I waste any time reading this chapter?' Before you skip this chapter completely I would like to challenge the underlying assumptions behind this statement. It assumes:

➤ you are advertising in media (print or broadcast) with national (or even international) coverage, across a wide spectrum of industries and subject interest
➤ you are advertising in order to persuade consumers of your product to respond immediately, or to make an immediate purchase of your products.

I maintain that neither assumption is necessarily true for you in your library so you should re-consider your perception of advertising and consider whether and how you could benefit from it.

If you were selling fast-moving consumer goods distributed through retail or mail order then these assumptions would be correct. You would anticipate selling thousands, or possibly millions of products to a large number of customers, making profits large enough to justify substantial spending on advertising.

But:

➤ you are marketing professional products and services to a closely-defined group of people
➤ your objectives in using advertising will not (usually) be to 'sell' your service directly from the page. Your customers are unlikely to see an advert then rush to place an order for your products immediately: they will want to ask questions of you, or request further information in the form of brochures or case studies. The customers' decision to buy (even if no money changes hands) is more complex. The advert is an invitation for the customer to start a relationship, not the catalyst for a quick sale
➤ your advertising objectives will be to raise awareness, provide information, establish or maintain your brand image or market position by providing points of difference between you and your competitors, launch a new service or remind customers what you do.

Therefore, if you can answer 'Yes' to the following questions, you should re-consider your views on advertising as a suitable tool for your marketing communications:

➤ can advertising help me achieve my marketing objectives?
➤ can I identify suitable media to reach my target market at an affordable price?

Advertising does some things very well

To help you answer the first question, advertising does some things very well:

➤ communication
➤ product or service focus
➤ brand image
➤ positioning
➤ brand loyalty and confidence
➤ selling
➤ marketing support.

Communication

Advertising can communicate information very effectively. If you want to inform your target market about, for example, the launch of a new online service, an open evening, lower pricing, or extended opening hours, then advertising in the right media gets the message across.

If you do not know the personal names and contact details for your target market then advertising is useful because it is a non-personalized method of communication. Once enquirers provide these details, they can be included in more personal, and perhaps more effective, methods of communication. For example, the following situations make initial contact via direct methods difficult or expensive:

➤ libraries with large market sectors (large public libraries)
➤ libraries with a clear understanding of their target market may lack the knowledge or resources to contact the appropriate individuals in an organization (a charity library)
➤ libraries widening their marketplace, perhaps for one particular service or product, (for example, a local library with a special collection and expertise in (say) transport might compile a bibliography of worldwide interest), advertising in appropriate media would be an effective way of reaching this market without attempting to make individual contact with thousands of people.

Product or service focus

Advertising can highlight specific aspects of your service. Because it is not the medium to communicate complex messages about your multifaceted library, it reinforces simple messages that distinguish you from your competitors. For example, advertising your library website in the company newsletter under the banner, 'Open all hours' specifically targets overseas staff who have often experienced problems accessing the corporate library across different time zones.

Brand image

Advertising can establish and reinforce your brand image. Once you have designed or chosen your logo for the library you will want to ensure

61

it gets in front of the people in your market sectors as quickly and effectively as possible. Advertising in media seen regularly by your potential customers increases the likelihood of achieving this. Branding helps customers build a bridge in their mind between your logo and your library. Once built they will use it time and time again, often without even realizing it, to recognize your library whenever they see the logo – on adverts, newsletters, brochures, letterheads, or websites.

Positioning

Advertising positions you against the competition. As well as promoting specific features of your service like better access, impartiality, or faster document delivery, advertising demonstrates that you are a serious player in the market. Even if your advert is just a black-and-white quarter page, it announces your intention to address the needs of your market and creates a more favourable impression than competing organizations that do not promote themselves, preferring to wait for customers to discover them by accident.

Brand loyalty and confidence

Advertising can help build customers' brand loyalty towards your library. They like to see adverts from their suppliers because it reinforces their decision to use your services. If your customers rely on the advice of intermediaries like consultants or other professional advisers, advertising can deflect fears that you are unknown in the market.

Selling

Advertising sells products. You cannot rule out the possibility of wanting to sell something, even if you currently run a free service. Specific items like publications, company searches, patent information, leaflets on specialist topics, CD-ROMs, or even subscriptions to online services can be effectively sold by advertising.

Marketing support

Advertising can be a useful tool for supporting other marketing methods, i.e. it can be used to support other promotions or campaigns using different marketing media. In this way you can advertise your presence at an exhibition, or in a magazine targeted at customers recently mail-shotted. The advert provides a valuable second 'hit' to reinforce the message carried by your 'front-line' medium.

Your target media

The second question posed above was: 'Can I identify suitable media to reach my target market at an affordable price?' Your collection of media packs from the exercise in the last chapter, identifying the print and broadcast media read by your target markets, will be a useful starting point, although the cost of advertising in some of these will remind you of the value of getting your information in their editorial pages free of charge!

Take care to read the media pack closely. Although colour pages may be too expensive for your budget, there will be cheaper options like small mono (black and white) adverts. You can also discuss your requirements with advertising staff in the media you would really like to advertise in. They have a financial interest in helping you afford to advertise and they might suggest something within your budget. Remember, no matter how hard they try to sell you something you cannot afford, you can always just say no.

In examining your media packs, you will probably realize you need to find different media that reach the same people but with less glossy or expensive publications. Perhaps there are magazines with a more local focus, or newsletters produced by special interest groups (these are not unique to the LIS profession), or even in-house magazines if you have large organizations within your potential customer base. Perhaps you can identify some websites regularly accessed by your target market and arrange some reciprocal links or advertising deals.

To share costs, you may need to seek strategic partners to work with you on joint campaigns. Your type of library and market sectors will determine the type of potential partner: local community organizations, training and enterprise bodies, local and central government agencies, companies in the private sector, even other libraries will all be useful partners. As long as they have an interest in reaching the same market sectors, but without having competitive products and services, collaboration can be a useful source of advice, expertise, and funding.

The successful advertisement

As you are unlikely to be spending your valuable marketing budget on expensive agencies to design your advertising, you will need to hone your DIY skills, and the place to start is in considering what constitutes a successful advert.

For your ad to be considered a success for any single reader it has to be:

➤ seen
➤ scanned
➤ read
➤ understood
➤ remembered
➤ easy to respond to.

Seen

If they do not look at the page where your ad appears, customers will be unable to respond to it. There is nothing much you can do about that, except to avoid advertising on pages which are likely to be ignored, which is not always possible. Always ask for the position you want (right-hand page facing editorial is normally regarded as favourite) as it can often be negotiated for free (the position, not the ad).

Scanned

When readers see an advert they make a split-second decision whether to read it. This is why consumer ads are 'eye-catching', with bold colours and design, stunning graphics or pictures, or even misleading text, to make you stop and stare. If you are already known to the readers then branding your ad with your logo will create instant recognition (over a period of time). Always include some graphics – text-only ads do not work and can even be counter-productive, making your organization appear one-dimensional and, dare I say it, boring.

Read

Although it is not possible to guarantee customers read the whole advert, you can make sure readers know what the advert is about in the first few words, and by using jargon-free direct language that persuades readers they need your products.

Understood

Adverts cannot carry complex messages because they have just a few seconds to persuade the reader. So you must compromise when writing ad copy – if you have six messages to communicate, accept that you will do well to get two of them over in a single ad. This is not the place for detail, however relevant it might be. Use the first person style of writing (use 'we' and 'you') and keep sentences and paragraphs short. Use questions in your headline and subheadings – 'Why do people look for information in the most unlikely places?', 'How would you find out where to . . .?', 'Do you always get the right answer when you ask the right question?', etc.

Remembered

Unless the reader is able to respond immediately s/he will bookmark the page so they are reminded to take action when it is more convenient. If your message is concise, relevant, using short memorable phrases, you will stand a better chance of being remembered. Sometimes customers will consult a magazine several months, or even years, old because they remembered a distinctive advert. This does not apply to loose leaf inserts, where you might 'insert' a brochure or flier into a particular issue. These have the advantage of having immediate impact because they tend to be scanned (and often read and understood) before the magazine itself is opened. But their strength is also their weakness – because they are loose they are often read by the first reader only, being filed, discarded or lost before other readers get the chance to see them. And if you remember a useful insert and look for it in six months time then it's a minor miracle if you can still find it!

Easy to respond to

Your address, telephone, and fax numbers are essential. If you have a website and e-mail address, include them too. If you can provide a contact name that's even better – customers like to feel they are contacting an identifiable person, even if they do not actually speak to that person when they call. If you anticipate customers wanting to respond by fax or post, then include a tear-off coupon for them to complete, if you have room on the ad. This is known as a response mechanism and can improve the response rates to adverts dramatically.

Now re-read the section above keeping our old friend AIDA in mind – seeing and scanning is all about getting attention, reading is about gaining readers' interest, understanding and remembering is about creating desire for your products and action requires an easy response mechanism.

This process is different for each individual and for each magazine but can be generally considered as a function of the publication, not the market. In other words, if you want to maximize the chances of your ad being seen, scanned, read, understood and remembered you must choose your advertising media carefully.

For example, you want to advertise in *Ferret fanciers weekly* but cannot afford the rates for display advertisements, where pages dedicated to advertising appear. You can, however, afford to take a classified ad in the same magazine – it's the same circulation, the same readership, with the same potential exposure for your ad, and much cheaper, so why not do it?

Why not, indeed? If you think your target market (not necessarily the typical reader) examines the classified ads then it is worth considering. But if your potential customers are likely to ignore the ten pages of small type at the back of the magazine every week, then it is not such a good idea.

When you have written/designed your advert, look at it and consider it from the customer's point of view and ask yourself how well it represents your library – does it look like the product of an organization you would want to deal with?

I once read the following sentence and it has always served me well:

**'Advertising says something about you . . .
be careful it doesn't say you're sad, skint and desperate!'**

Exercise

List all the publications you would advertise in if you had the budget. This list will be useful in all your future marketing communications, especially for PR activity.

Using the guidelines above, design an A4-sized advert in mono (black and white), using the best technology available to you. If all you have is a word processor, then that will be fine.

Display the finished ad prominently in your library or information unit.

Design a short survey form so you can randomly ask visitors to the library whether they:

➤ saw it
➤ read it
➤ understood it
➤ liked it.

If any of the answers are 'No' then ask for the reasons.

Whatever else you do with the results of this exercise, even if you never have the funds to place your advert in a publication, you will learn a lot about how customers perceive communications that you first thought were models of clarity, simplicity, and brevity!

Summary

➤ **Advertising is not necessarily too expensive for libraries**
➤ **Choose your media carefully**
➤ **Be clear about your objectives.**

Chapter 6
Direct mail

In this chapter you'll find out:

➤ why direct mail works
➤ how to develop a strategy for list development
➤ how to overcome practical difficulties.

What is direct mail?

Depending on your point of view, direct mail is either junk mail or advertising by post. It is a marketing communication sent to customers and potential customers identified as members of a market sector, consisting of a letter specific to that sector, enclosures, and an offer or inducement to respond. It is normally:

➤ personalized – in that it is sent to named individuals
➤ unsolicited
➤ sent by post.

The three planks of successful direct mail are the list, the offer, and the copy (the words and pictures you use on your letter and enclosed information) and the first of these is by far the most important. No matter how good an offer you make, or how well it is presented, if it is not seen by the right person, then you have wasted your time and effort.

Your strategy for list development

To get the right names you need to build lists of customers and potential customers in a format that will enable you to produce mailshot letters quickly and easily – in other words a basic marketing database. Start by recording names and contact details only – collect other information which will prove useful at a later date. For example, if I am on your database you might hold the following information on me:

- name
- job title
- department
- address
- telephone
- fax
- e-mail
- website address (URL)
- nature of organization
- market sector (am I staff, student, businessperson, journalist?)
- professional interests
- miscellaneous notes.

This marketing intelligence allows you to send me direct mail for a variety of reasons:

- I live in a town or county or postcode that you are targeting
- I have the right job title
- my organization type is one of your target markets, or you have already classified me according to your own market segmentation
- there is something in my record that fits a particular mailing requirement – for example, you are inviting individuals interested in doing business in Europe to a seminar or workshop
- or combinations of these – for example, I have the word 'marketing' in my job title and I have an e-mail address.

Note that, as you will be holding personal details about individuals (their home or work details are classified as personal information), your organization will need to be registered under the Data Protection Act.

No matter how much knowledge you already have about your customers you will always need to acquire more, and you will need to keep your existing records up-to-date. This is a time-consuming task that will involve the use of both internal and external sources:

Internal sources

- ➤ customer lists
- ➤ loan records
- ➤ library enquiry forms
- ➤ correspondence
- ➤ internal telephone directory
- ➤ intranet
- ➤ staff newsletters
- ➤ colleagues inside and outside the library.

External sources

- ➤ list brokers
- ➤ telephone directories
- ➤ trade directories and yearbooks
- ➤ newspapers, magazines, journals – editorial and advertising, paying particular attention to changes in personnel and recruitment adverts: a new person in charge at a potential customer organization often presents a good opportunity to establish a new relationship
- ➤ online databases containing news, company information, economic and social trends
- ➤ the Internet
- ➤ TV and radio – news and advertising reveal trends in your market sectors
- ➤ colleagues in other organizations often provide useful information at meetings of special interest groups, seminars, workshops, and social events
- ➤ competitors' marketing material reveals information about their own customer base through lists or individual case studies; seemingly satisfied customers of a competitor are often happy to receive material about new ideas or alternative approaches.

> ## Exercise
>
> Choose six newspapers or magazines that are relevant to your marketplace. Scan them for information about organizations and individuals and record any details you would want to include in your marketing database.

Why should libraries use direct mail?

Direct mail works because it helps customers understand your messages in ways that other marketing tools cannot, because it is:

- ➤ personal
- ➤ highly focused
- ➤ easy to control and measure
- ➤ economical.

Personal

It is *personal* because it is addressed to an individual. Sending your messages to correctly named individuals is important because the alternative is sending mail to wrongly-named individuals (ouch!) or with the general salutation 'Dear Job Title', or 'Dear Sir'. These compromises increase the chance of your material being consigned to the waste-basket before it is read.

Highly focused and easy to control

It is *highly focused* because it is under your control. You can ensure the message has been tailored to reflect the needs of the recipient, using text that is as brief or as comprehensive as it needs to be.

Direct mail is not just 'advertising by post' because it can be used to *communicate more complex messages*. As well as using the letter (which, contrary to a popular marketing myth, can be more than one side of A4 if necessary) you can enclose leaflets, brochures, newsletters, bulletins, and client profiles.

Direct mail often works best in *achieving objectives that can be expressed in terms of a specific offer with a cut-off date*. Giving incentives to (for example) attend seminars, workshops or open days, or offering discounts on publication sales, are effective because you are asking a closed question requiring a 'Yes' or 'No' answer. A cut-off date concentrates the mind of the recipient and speeds response.

Easy to measure

The success of your mailing is *easy to measure* because the response tends to come in quickly or not at all. Within four or five weeks (and often much earlier) you will have received the vast majority of responses you will ever get.

Direct mail is *less public* than other marketing tools. The message is sent to a specific individual, in contrast to advertising and PR communications. If you are in a competitive environment make sure you see your competitors' mailings. Ask colleagues for copies, and get on mailing lists.

For some organizations (especially those in the public sector), adverts and press releases are often subject to a slow, bureaucratic process of approval. As it is less public, direct mail is seldom subject to the same restrictions and offers libraries in these bodies a flexible alternative.

Pilot mailings

If you have a large market sector and you want to mailshot thousands of people it is advisable to first *conduct a pilot mailing*, sending your material to a small number of respondents to evaluate response and decide where improvements can be made. This is easy with direct mail – choose a representative sample from your database and send your mailing to a handful of people. Follow it up by telephone to ask recipients if they remember receiving it, and to check their understanding of the messages, especially the offer. You can improve the effectiveness of your direct mail activity by listening to your customers this way, before committing substantial resources. This is not possible when using other marketing tools.

Economical

Finally, direct mail is *economical*. For the price of printing a few leaflets and a second class stamp you can communicate directly with individuals known to be prime targets for the services offered by your library.

Direct mail can be used to . . .

Direct mail can be used to:

- ➤ launch a new product or service
- ➤ test services on a new market sector
- ➤ target new customers
- ➤ invite customers to an event (seminar, open day, library tour, exhibition)
- ➤ sell products
- ➤ inform your markets of relevant and topical news.

So why don't all libraries use direct mail to promote themselves? As you suspect, there are some problems associated with it and it is best to be aware of these from the beginning.

Potential problems and how to avoid them

The major potential problems to avoid are:

- ➤ junk mail
- ➤ lack of time (maintaining lists)
- ➤ lack of time (mailing out).

Problem 1 – junk mail

Direct mail has a poor image. Much unsolicited mail is perceived by recipients to be 'junk mail' and given very little attention, so how can you ensure that your mailings are welcomed rather than tolerated, and read rather than discarded?

Here is the answer:

- ➤ get your list right
- ➤ brand it
- ➤ make an offer
- ➤ do something different.

Get your list right

The term ' junk mail ' is rarely a criticism of the quality of the mailer itself, but often reflects the fact that it has been sent to the wrong person.

For example, if you are the library manager in an industrial/commercial library and receive a mailshot promoting a conference on the benefits of Java programming skills in building your company intranet, then the quality of the mailing doesn't count. It goes straight in the waste-basket because it has been sent to the wrong person.

If you cannot identify the appropriate individual(s) in your targeted market sectors, preferably by name and not just job title, do not send anything. Not only does it waste your time and effort but the very nature of direct mail is to repeat this error time and time again, compounding the waste and giving a poor image of your organization.

Brand it

Before your mailings can be welcomed they must be recognized. Strong branding leads to instant recognition which by itself is enough to make your mailing stand out.

You can also make recipients feel special and reinforce customer loyalty by giving a name to your specific services. For example, if you send newsletters to customers every month, be explicit – point out that this is a monthly service provided free of charge and available only to current customers. Give this service a name like 'the (your name) Library News Club'.

Make an offer

Mailings that do not explicitly require a response are more likely to be regarded as junk mail because they do not answer the main question going through the mind of the recipient as they read the first few words of your letter – 'What's in it for me?'

Mailings without offers are less likely to get a response because this question goes unanswered. If you want to send mailshots with the objective of providing information and raising awareness, with no specific offer, try to think of something you can offer to anyone who wants to find out more about your library – more detailed information, an appointment to discuss their needs, a free hour online, a tour of the library – anything that says what's in it for them if they respond.

Do something different

Although most direct mail consists of a covering letter with various enclosures, you could use some creativity to distinguish your material from the rest. Have a brainstorming session to generate new ideas to get your message across in a novel way. Some of them are bound to be afford-able!

For example, have you considered sending birthday cards for unusual and seldom celebrated anniversaries – to customers on their first anniversary, to lapsed customers one year after they last used the library, to customers with anniversaries coming up themselves?

Problem 2 – lack of time (lists)

Direct mail is a labour-intensive activity. Maintaining a marketing data-base could take many hours each and every week. Decide how much time is required to perform this task, remembering that the governing factor is the pace of change in your market sectors rather than the market size.

For example, a public library will have some markets that are large but change very slowly, or at regular and predictable intervals. List maintenance for distance learners could be a quarterly or semi-annual activity.

An industrial/commercial library in the financial or legal sector may have market sectors containing relatively few organizations, each with many departments and a high staff turnover. List maintenance would be required at least once per month, maybe even weekly.

Once you know the size of the task you can allocate staff to scan inter-nal and external resources and update your database. If you have a resource problem then make it a task that rotates every week/month/quar-ter. In a small library with (say) three staff, updating their marketing data-base every quarter, each member of staff would be responsible for list management once every nine months – not an intolerable burden.

If you are a solo librarian, any extra work causes a resource problem. My recommendation would be to keep a manual file for notes of changes you want to make to the marketing database throughout the week, updating the database itself at one pre-determined day and time in the week. Although this seems a high frequency it keeps the time taken to complete the task to a minimum and you will come to see it as a quick 10 or 15 minute task at the end of each week which pays dividends when you get the time to put some mailshots together.

Problem 2 – lack of time (mailing out)

It will take time to send out your mailshots – collating marketing material, stuffing envelopes, etc. – but it can be kept to a minimum by preparing mailing packs well in advance. Whenever your own clerical staff have some free time, or whenever you are asked to provide some tasks for office juniors, or for temporary staff between other jobs, ask them to collate some marketing packs in window envelopes.

When material is needed for individual inquirers, or for direct mail activities, you need only insert letters (with any new items) and they can be sealed, stamped and posted with minimum effort.

How might our case study libraries use direct mail in their marketing communications?

Case study 1: A public library targeting local small businesses

Monthly
Newsletter with topical business information news, especially new acquisitions, and schedule of library tours and open evenings.

Quarterly
The next quarter's events as supported by the library in conjunction with other agencies.
Other specific mailings are planned for the year April–March as follows, although changes may be made:

April
Special invitations to workshops on self-assessment taxation, in conjunction with a local accounting firm.

Continued

June
Letter on the value of company information, with order forms for Companies House search service offering discount for all orders received by end of July.

September
To coincide with the planned acquisition of Patents information on CD-ROM, send a brief letter to technical/research and development managers explaining patent and trademark law and offering free demonstrations of the CD-ROM at the library's 'Patently Yours' evenings.

December
Send a letter on the importance of market research to small businesses with client profile, a flier on library sources for market research, and an offer of a discounted book on the subject (as agreed with local bookshop).

Case study 2: Academic library targeting part-time students

Mailings each term will include library newsletters, new acquisitions, current awareness bulletins, etc. addressed to individual students but to save postage they will be delivered to lecture-rooms. This is known as a maildrop – a direct mailing that is delivered free of charge, or at very low cost.

Other specific mailings will include:

September
An introductory letter stressing the ways in which the library can help part-time students, enclosing a leaflet about opening hours highlighting evening, weekend and holiday-time access, and invitation to library tours with a prize draw (book token) for each new registration before end of October.

December
Letter explaining opening times over the Christmas holiday offering free Internet tuition.

March
A mailing that is one part promotion and one part market research. Ask for questionnaires to be completed (another prize draw?) to get feedback on your success during the year, and promote training sessions in library on 'Exams for Beginners'.

Case study 3: Industrial/commercial library targeting the Board of Directors

This market sector is internal so mailings will be sent via the internal mail (snail mail and e-mail) to provide library services (bulletins, newsletters, journal contents, daily press items of interest) as well as 'unsolicited' promotions:

Quarterly
Send a special 'strategic' edition of the current awareness bulletin, drawing attention to books, journal articles, CD-ROMS, Internet sites of topical and strategic importance to the company.

January
Send a letter explaining the new services/activities anticipated in the coming year in the library, suggesting a short meeting to discuss any ideas they might have, and to discuss their own personal requirements.

March
Send a letter with brief explanation of developments in knowledge management, offering a more comprehensive analysis in the form of a presentation to a future board meeting.

September
It's time to lobby for next year's library budget – send a letter reporting some of the year's successes enclosing client profiles from each director's division.

November
Having ordered the required number of copies of the Chancellor's Budget Statement from the Bank of England, and taken personal delivery of them on the day of the speech, send a copy with a brief letter to each director. Make sure they receive it as soon as possible (just minutes after the Chancellor has sat down would be good) and make sure they know it was the library's initiative.

Case study 4: Medical charity library targeting the media

Given the target market, most mailings will be closely aligned with PR activity.

January
Letter inviting media to press launch of the 'front page' service, with leaflet containing full details, and offer exclusive interview with a celebrity supporter of the charity, to be drawn from all attendees.

April
Letter stressing the need to keep up-to-date with developments in the field, launching the new website and FAQ pages. To draw attention to the 'do you know?' page, where queries can be keyed onto the web page and sent by e-mail, offer a challenge – 'Ask a question we can't answer and win a bottle of bubbly!'

September
Letter emphasizing the importance of the media to the charity, launching 'dedicated' fax numbers and e-mail addresses for rapid response to queries, requests for quotes, and interview requests. Offer library tour and interview with the Director to the first five users of the lines.

Summary

➤ Get your list right
➤ Make an offer
➤ Make the time to do it.

Chapter 7
Exhibitions

Summary

In this chapter you'll find out:

➤ **what to look for when considering exhibiting**
➤ **tips on exhibiting**
➤ **the difference between exhibitions, seminars, roadshows, etc.**

Why don't libraries exhibit more?

Libraries do not use exhibitions to market themselves very often because they are time-consuming, expensive and difficult to evaluate.

➤ exhibitions are *time-consuming* because they require a lot of planning and work before the event takes place, and once you get there it takes at least one person (and perhaps more) out of the library for the duration of the exhibition
➤ exhibitions are *expensive* – the exhibition space itself is just one of the many costs involved
➤ exhibitions are often *difficult to evaluate* because success can only be measured by enquiries received on the stand. It is impossible to assess whether your messages were successfully conveyed to those who did not make it onto your stand, despite the fact that many visitors might have intended to speak to you but never made it. Many more will have read your listing in the catalogue on the way home and regretted missing the chance to find out more.

Why should you consider it?

In some of your market sectors there will be one or two exhibitions every year that provide a focal point, bringing your targeted individuals together in one place with the specific intention of evaluating new products and services, and new suppliers.

You may have customers you only communicate with by telephone or e-mail. At exhibitions you can meet them face-to-face. You can ask questions, answer queries, demonstrate your products and services, and discuss issues and ideas. This helps build personal relationships, leaving a stronger impression than your PR, advertising or direct mail activities can.

You can meet representatives from other exhibitors, who are either potential customers or possibly partners in joint marketing activities. Your shared objectives give you an instant rapport. You can use this to your advantage by exploring ideas with people who are normally difficult to reach (especially face-to-face) because they are busy with their own customers.

Exhibiting demonstrates that you are a serious player in the market. You are prepared to commit time, effort and money to reach the right people. When they recall the stands of their major suppliers they will remember your stand amongst them.

Attendance at an exhibition can be used in other forms of promotion:

➤ press releases provide news of your presence before the event, and promote your success afterwards
➤ advertising can carry an extra slogan ('see us on Stand 123')
➤ direct mail promotes the exhibition and distributes tickets, and publicizes any incentive you have offered ('your business card could win a free publication').

Our case study libraries all have a different approach in their use of exhibitions:

Case study 1: Public library targeting local small business

There are about a dozen exhibitions aimed at this market sector and the budget allows attendance of just two, so the choice is always difficult. This year the intention is to go to one general show and one event that is aimed at a sector which has been slow to respond to previous marketing efforts – manufacturing industry.

The Southern Manufacturing Show is to be held over two days in February at Thorpe Park, Surrey. In addition to the exhibition stand, the library will make a contribution to the free seminar programme with a session entitled 'Information for engineers – where to go and how to use it'.

The Surrey Business Showcase, the largest business-to-business exhibition in the county, is to be held over two days at Sandown Park at the end of June. A 25% discount has been negotiated with the organizers in return for offering specific information services to visitors and exhibitors. The library will contribute to a joint seminar session (with the local Business Link) on 'Getting money out of Europe for YOUR business'.

There will also be numerous opportunities to use the library's display equipment when giving talks to local small business clubs and chambers of commerce throughout the year.

Case study 2: Academic library targeting part-time students

There is only one focal point of the year where an exhibition stand of any kind could be used to promote the library – the enrolment days and evenings in late August and early September. If the library are successful in borrowing display equipment for this, then at least one member of staff will be present throughout enrolment to promote the library services.

> ### Case study 3: Industrial/commercial library targeting the main Board of Directors
>
> Although exhibitions are not very useful in reaching this market sector, some portable display equipment has been purchased to support the marketing activities aimed at middle managers, especially those in UK locations outside head office.
>
> The library manager visits these sites as often as possible and can now offer to set up a lunchtime or evening exhibition stand to demonstrate services using a laptop computer and a large monitor borrowed from the site. This will raise awareness of the library with a broader group of people than is possible with pre-arranged appointments with specific individuals throughout the working day.

> ### Case study 4: Medical charity library targeting the media
>
> Exhibitions are not very useful for reaching this market sector although the Information Services Manager is in close contact with the marketing department to ensure that literature about the library is available when they exhibit at health shows throughout the year.
>
> Display equipment will be borrowed for use at the press launch days of the new front page service, and the new website facilities for the media.

If you do exhibit

If you can afford to exhibit you should make sure the following questions are answered.

Is this the right exhibition to attend?

There will be many opportunities to exhibit throughout the year and you will not have sufficient resources to attend them all. Therefore you need to choose the one or two that you can afford with great care.

You must first of all satisfy yourself that the exhibition will attract the right type of visitor. Ask for details of attendance over the last two or three years. Will individuals from your targeted market sector be attending in any numbers? Ask your current customers and competitors whether they will be going, and if not, then why not. Who will be attending – end users or decision-makers?

How will the organizer attract visitors to the exhibition? Are they actively marketing it or do they expect everyone to know about it already? How will free tickets be distributed – by direct mail, inserts in magazines? Inadequate marketing by the organizer can reduce visitor numbers, making the event less useful to your library.

If you are happy that the exhibition will attract the right people, examine the dates of the show. Is the time of year appropriate for visitors? Do the dates clash with other events? Look out for school holidays (especially half-terms), major sporting events, the likelihood of bad weather, or anything that might have a detrimental effect on attendance.

Another important factor is the attractiveness or convenience of the location. Is it easy to reach, especially by public transport?

How much will it (really) cost me?

The exhibition sales brochure will provide the cost of exhibiting in £s per square metre of space. This price (which is rarely set in stone – it is negotiable, especially near the event date when organizers will want to avoid empty spaces) is just the start – there are many additional costs to be considered:

space-only stands are just that – an empty space in the hall. You will need to pay for:

➤ electric sockets (for personal computers)
➤ telephone lines (to access the Internet)
➤ furniture hire (tables, chairs, etc.)
➤ carpeting hire
➤ catering (if you are offering refreshments, remembering that most exhibition organizers will not allow you to take your own food or drink – you will have to buy it from them, at their prices).

a 'shell scheme' provides a space with some facilities included, such as signs, a table and chair, and one electric socket. Other requirements will need to be priced:

➤ your own equipment will need to be bought or hired (display stands, display boards with your name/logo/message, computers, large screen monitors, literature holders, etc.)

➤ transport to/from exhibition to set up and return your equipment

➤ accommodation and/or subsistence for staff manning the stand

➤ transport to/from exhibition for staff

➤ promoting the stand at the exhibition itself (literature on exhibition buses, posters in the car park).

How do I maximize attendance on my stand?

Use all the marketing tools at your disposal to publicize your attendance, starting with your free entry in the exhibitors catalogue.

Send press releases to your target press and broadcast media so that it reaches them in time for the preview issue that is published two or three weeks before the event, giving readers time to schedule attendance in their diaries. Sometimes trade journals will preview a particular show to highlight new products or services coming onto the market. Talk to the Editor to find out if they can give your library a paragraph or two in the preview.

Prepare a press pack containing a press release, newsletter, brochure, leaflets, and/or client profiles to leave in the press office at the exhibition itself, and make sure you deliver it before the show opens to visitors. This gets your information to all journalists in attendance, even those who do not make it to your stand.

If you are placing adverts anywhere, make sure they mention the exhibition name, dates and location, with your stand number.

Use direct mail to distribute free tickets to individuals in your marketing database about three weeks beforehand, publicizing any special offers you are making to visitors.

Announce your attendance on all correspondence for the month preceding the exhibition, either on a specially printed colour stick-on label, or by adding a P.S. in bold or colour ('See us on Stand 123'). Don't forget to publicize the event on your website.

How do I present the right image on the stand itself?

Look welcoming and enthusiastic at all times. This is not as easy as it sounds – over two or three long working days in front of customers every minute of every hour there are bound to be times when you feel tired and bored – do your best not to show it.

Approach people in a friendly, professional manner (avoiding the 'exhibition pounce'). Practice some opening phrases other than 'Can I help you?' If formed as a question, they should be open and not closed questions. Most customers will be reluctant to start the conversation, for fear of the 'hard sell', so think of it as a friendly conversation between colleagues where you have to start the ball rolling.

When you are the only person on the stand, avoid resembling a security guard on patrol (hands behind back, blocking the view of exhibits or display boards, staring into space).

The rule on the stand is no smoking, no drinking, and no slouching – under any circumstances. If you are in doubt, imagine you are making a presentation to customers and being observed by your chief executive. Would they approve? If not, don't do it, whatever it is.

Offer prizes for business cards or completed enquiry forms placed in a box on the stand. It helps collect the names of people who had neither the time or inclination to speak to you directly.

If you talk to someone, always exchange contact details – you can add them to your marketing database and increase the enquiry count that will be used to justify your attendance. Try to give every genuine visitor something about your services – even if they claim to 'know all about you', persuade them that at least one promotional item on the stand is hot off the press.

When it's all over . . .

➤ Have a de-briefing. Discuss what worked and what didn't, making sure that next time you build on your strengths and improve on your weaknesses.

➤ Follow up the visitors to your stand. Send a letter two or three days later, thanking them for visiting your stand, letting them know how successful the exhibition was for you, and enclosing a recent leaflet or newsletter. Even if they already have a copy, it will serve as a useful reminder of their visit.

➤ Analyse the enquiries you received. Are there significant trends that point towards changes or improvements you can make in your library? Is the market asking for something new? Identify visitors that were 'hot to trot' – those who wanted something specific from you right now – and take immediate action.

➤ Ask the organizers if they can provide a mailing list of all visitors – sometimes this is surprisingly inexpensive.

➤ Write a brief report outlining costs and benefits of attendance, partly for your own use when you are considering attendance next year, and partly to publicize your success to colleagues and managers. Circulate it to all the colleagues who helped with preparations, with a thank-you letter. They will appreciate knowing how well you did.

DIY exhibitions, seminars and roadshows

These can all be effective ways of promoting your library but they have various advantages and disadvantages.

It is easy to forget that DIY events have no organizer to make sure everything runs smoothly – it's all your responsibility. And similarly, you will have to do your own marketing to attract visitors or delegates. This extra work and cost can be reduced by organizing events in partnership with other organizations targeting customers in the same market sectors.

These events are less independent – it will be obvious to potential visitors that they will only get to see your products and services on display so from their perspective it is more akin to a sales appointment. They will expect to be 'sold' your library and if that doesn't interest them at the specific moment they receive your publicity then they will not come. It may also be more difficult to justify time away from their own office if they cannot show they are attending an industry-wide event.

Therefore the visitors coming to your events will be fewer in number but probably higher in quality i.e., they will be more interested in what you have to say by virtue of their agreement to come along.

Your own events can be more focused towards the specific messages you want to convey because you will get more time and attention from

each visitor. This increases the value of the event because you will probably get more information from them, have the time to address their
questions in substantial detail, and be able to build even stronger relationships. Conversely, some visitors might be more tight-lipped because
they feel they are in a sales situation rather than at an exhibition.

It might be less costly to organize events of your own, but it might
not. If this is an important factor, examine all the costs and be sure that
you are saving money before committing resources.

Summary

➤ Consider the costs carefully before making your decision
➤ Make sure everyone knows you are attending
➤ Follow up all enquiries, especially those who ask for some specific
action.

Chapter 8
Why should you invest time evaluating your marketing activities?

> **In this chapter you'll find out:**
>
> ➤ why evaluation is important
> ➤ how to measure success and failure.

Of all the pressing demands on your time perhaps the least appealing is the task of evaluating the success of past (and present) activities. When you are being hounded to complete ever more tasks, why make time to look back at the ones you managed to get round to, those that you now regard as finished?

There are three good reasons for questioning how well you have done:

➤ if you don't, someone else will
➤ success should be built on
➤ mistakes should be rectified, areas of weakness should be improved.

If you don't, someone else will

In practical terms you have no real choice whether to evaluate or not, because if you don't, someone else will do it on your behalf. No matter how successful you are, there will come the day when your managers or funders want to measure the success of your marketing activities.

So the real choice is between conducting your own evaluation, using objectives outlined in your marketing plan as the benchmark for success, or waiting for someone else to do it for you, using standards of performance that you may not be aware of and so will be unable to meet.

Success should be built on

Evaluation and consequent identification of your success allows you to:

➤ tell your customers – publicize the fact that you had 50 enquiries from your exhibition, or that 75% of delegates to your seminar programme became loyal customers within three months; include news of your success in newsletter articles, press releases, direct mail and your website

➤ tell your funders – the effectiveness of your marketing confirms their faith in you and smooths the path when justifying your plans for next year.

And having identified the marketing activities that work best for you, make sure you repeat them again, and again, and again!

Mistakes and weaknesses

Evaluation will uncover mistakes and weaknesses in both your marketing planning and communications. Once identified, improvements can be made. For example:

➤ Your marketing plan was written to a tight deadline that left no time for a comprehensive segmentation of your different market sectors. Your plan identified three sectors, outlining the tools and messages you would use for each one. You now realize that one of these sectors contains two types of customer with completely different needs that require different approaches. Amend the marketing plan to keep it up-to-date, ensuring it reflects the current situation and continues to be an effective planning tool.

➤ You have identified a particular trade journal as one of your strategic targets and after initial success with press releases, your evaluation process highlights that none of your material has been published for the last six months. Further investigation reveals that the Editor has been working on a special project and has delegated day-to-day editorial responsibilities to the deputy editor. You can now build a relationship with this new contact, re-establishing the PR credibility of your organization.

In short, corrective action cannot be taken unless mistakes are identified and weaknesses exposed.

How to measure your success

There are three specific actions you can take to make it easy to measure your success:

➤ quantify your objectives
➤ build your measurement and evaluation methods into your marketing plan and your schedule
➤ find out why new customers approach you.

Quantify your objectives

Quantifying your objectives makes evaluation easy because it provides specific targets and standards of performance to measure against. All objectives can be quantified, even if they initially appear to be too general or vague. For example, to quantify the objective to 'raise awareness among local business' you will need to analyse in detail:

➤ the specific market sector(s) you want to reach; you will need to define them carefully to make subsequent evaluation easy – in this example you might use the geographical location of the customer and the job title(s) of individuals
➤ how you will measure raised awareness and the benchmarks of success
➤ how you can quantify this objective: the trick is to aim for improvement but avoid setting targets that are too ambitious; if you want to make sure that all local managing directors need to know about your business information service you may have to find out whether this can be realistically achieved in one year and how many of them already have this knowledge.

In this way the bland objective 'to raise awareness' can be transformed into something more meaningful and easy to measure such as 'to increase by 10% the number of directors (managing, sales, financial, technical, and production) of small businesses with annual turnover of less than £2 million in the Boroughs of Hart and Rushmoor in north-east Hampshire that, when asked where they can go for business information, will name this library.'

Build in measurement and evaluation methods

Build your measurement and evaluation methods into the marketing plan and your schedule. For example, stipulate that you will select 50 companies at random from your marketing database, ask them where they would go for their business information, and record the number that mention your library (unprompted). You will repeat this survey ten months later (just in time for your annual marketing report) to measure progress towards your target.

Find out why new customers approach you

Design a brief form to record the names and contact details of new customers or enquirers, including how they found out about you. Was it an item in the press, a mailshot sent three months ago, an exhibition catalogue passed on by a colleague, an advert in the local small business club newsletter, or word-of-mouth recommendation? Keep these forms near every telephone to make sure you remember to complete them. These are the input forms for your marketing database (see Chapter 6).

When analysed over a period of time, they will provide a count of positive responses to specific marketing activities but these numbers are not the only measure of your success. This device cannot provide information about the number of people who have received something from you, were impressed and interested, and intend to contact you at a later date, and does not help you to evaluate individual pieces of marketing material.

Evaluation methods

There are several different ways to ask customers and potential customers for their opinions and perceptions of your marketing activities, each with their own advantages and disadvantages. If you have access to anyone with specialist skills in market research – designing questionnaires, conducting interviews, etc. – it would be worthwhile asking for their professional advice. Their expertise will help you extract a better quality of information from respondents in a form that can be readily used to measure and compare results.

It can be difficult to persuade people to spend time giving you their opinions, so offer an incentive to take part in evaluation surveys. Offering a prize draw for a product related to your library (for example, a free seminar place or discounted company search) is helpful but there is the chance that only individuals interested in the offered product will respond. This will not necessarily increase response rates and might even skew your results as the sample of respondents becomes self-selecting.

For these reasons, consider offering generally attractive prizes like bottles of champagne, boxes of chocolates, or flowers sent to a friend. Having more than one prize also means more winners, which will also increase the number of responses.

Evaluation methods

Advantages	Disadvantages
Postal/fax/e-mail survey form	
➤ reaches many people	➤ structured and mostly closed questions
➤ inexpensive	
➤ easy to compare results over time	➤ inflexible – little opportunity to deviate from standard questions
➤ it is claimed that people are more truthful in postal surveys than in face-to-face interviews	
➤ marketing material can be enclosed	➤ easy to be less truthful (no body language to read)
	➤ low response rate – 10% is high
Telephone survey	
➤ greater number of open questions	➤ labour intensive
➤ flexible – can deviate from structured format	➤ difficult to contact people at a convenient time
➤ rapid response	➤ cannot show example of marketing material

Continued

Face-to-face interview
- open questions
- flexible – can deviate from structured format
- interviewee's queries can be answered
- body language can be noted
- marketing material can be shown, and compared with competitors' material

- very labour-intensive
- only possible for small numbers
- concerns about confidentiality
- difficult to get customers to attend

Focus groups or customer panels
- all the advantages of face-to-face interviews plus
- more commitment from interviewees so true picture tends to emerge

- requires more skill to facilitate a group discussion
- difficult for leader to maintain neutrality
- difficult to get customers to attend

These are formal methods of evaluating your marketing activity. Sometimes the most useful feedback comes from conversations with customers and colleagues in informal settings that allow you to ask open, non-threatening questions like:

- What did you think of our latest newsletter/client profile/mailshot/advert?
- Why don't you use my library?

You will often get surprising answers (both positive and negative) that can be fed straight back into your marketing programmes.

Summary

- Get your evaluation in first
- Use it to keep your plans up-to-date
- Don't be afraid of criticism – this is a learning curve.

Further reading

This book was written mainly from my own experience but the following books and articles were useful:

Especially useful

Although these books were written for charities and voluntary organizations, they are practical, down-to-earth guides that build on the concepts introduced in this book.

Ali, Moi, *The DIY guide to marketing for charities and voluntary organisations*, London, The Directory of Social Change, 1996.

Ali, Moi, *The DIY guide to public relations for charities, voluntary organisations and community groups*, London, The Directory of Social Change, 1995.

Main list

Anderson, Alan H. and Kleiner, David, *Effective marketing communications: a skills and activity-based approach*, Oxford, Blackwell, 1995.

Batchelor, Bridget, 'Marketing the information service', in Scammell, Alison, (ed.), *Handbook of special librarianship and information work*, 7th edn, London, Aslib 1997.

Coote, Helen and Batchelor, Bridget, *How to market your library service effectively*, 2nd edn, London, Aslib, 1998.

Cronin, Blaise (ed.), *Marketing of library and information services*, London, Aslib, 1992.

Drucker, Peter, *Managing the non-profit organization*, London, Butterworth-Heinemann, 1990.

Duncan, Moira, 'How not to write a press release' in *Managing information*, 1 (9), September 1994, 39–40.

Duncan, Moira, 'Promotion through the press' in *Managing information*, 4 (6), July/August 1997, 37–39.

Fraser-Robinson, John, with Mosscroft, Pip, *Total quality marketing: what has to come next in sales, marketing and advertising*, London, Kogan Page, 1991.

Jefkins, Frank, *Advertising*, 3rd edn, London, Pitman Publishing, 1994.

Kotler, Philip and Andreason, Alan R., *Strategic marketing for non profit organizations*, 5th edn, New Jersey, Prentice-Hall, 1996.

de Saez, Eileen Elliott, *Marketing concepts for libraries and information services*, London, Library Association, 1997.

Sutherland, John and Gross, Nigel, *Marketing in action*, London, Pitman Publishing, 1991.

Motivational books

When you need new ideas but you are not in a very creative frame of mind, books like these help get the enthusiasm back. Everyone is motivated by different styles and different authors, but I found these uplifting. Although the first book is ostensibly about self-employment, it's all about marketing.

Burch, Geoff, *Go it alone! The streetwise secrets of self-employment*, London, Thorsons, 1997.

Forsyth, Patrick, *Everything you need to know about marketing*, 2nd edn, London, Kogan Page, 1996.

Prushan, Victor H., *No-nonsense marketing: 101 practical ways to win and keep customers*, New York, John Wiley, 1997.

Index

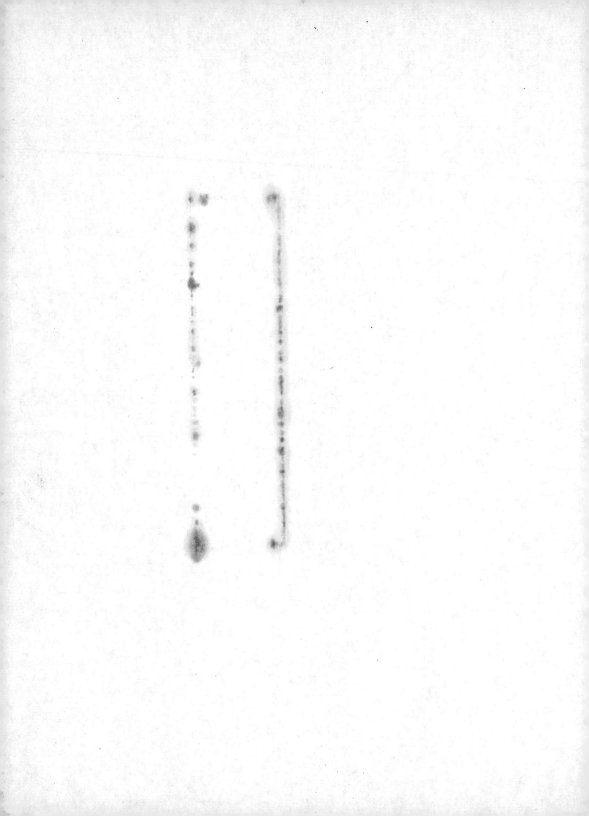